Hiker's Guide
to the
Mountains of Vermont

Jared Gange

Published by Huntington Graphics
Huntington, Vermont

Photo credits
Cover: Looking north from Camel's Hump, Jared Gange
Inset photo, back cover: Jared Gange
Title photo: Maple Ridge on Mt. Mansfield, Lars Gange
Pages 61 and 91: Matthew Cull
Page 95: Babben Enger
Page 79: Lars Gange
Pages 13, 19, 39, 51, 83: Jared Gange
Pages 56 and 71: Jerry LeBlond
Page 14: Andrew Nemethy
Page 9: Alden Pellett
Page 33: Nuna Teal Rood

Graphic design, maps, and typesetting
John A. Hadden, Resting Lion Studio, Huntington, Vermont

Editing
Assistant Editor, Linda Young

Publication Data

Gange, Jared
> **Hiker's Guide to the Mountains of Vermont**
> Includes index.
> ISBN 1-886064-03-2
Copyright 1996, Huntington Graphics
All rights reserved
Printed in the United States of America

Second edition

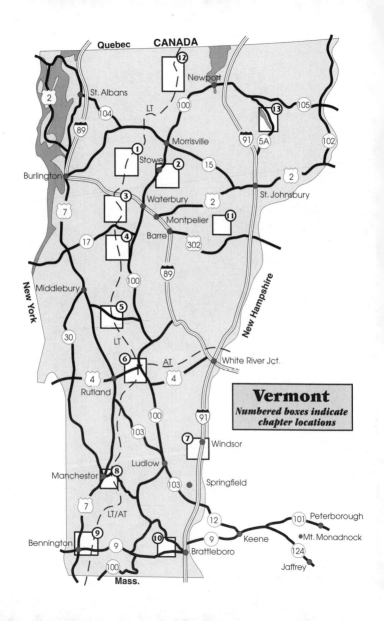

Quebec   **CANADA**

Newport

St. Albans

104

89

Morrisville

91 5A

105

102

(1) Stowe

(2)

15

St. Johnsbury

Burlington

7

(3)

Waterbury

2

2

Montpelier

(11)

17

(4)

Barre

302

100

89

New Hampshire

Middlebury

(5)

LT

30

(6)

AT

White River Jct.

4

4

Rutland

100

91

103

(7) Windsor

Ludlow

Springfield

Manchester (8)

103

Vermont
*Numbered boxes indicate
chapter locations*

7

LT/AT

(9)

101 Peterborough

Bennington

9

(10)

12

Keene

Mt. Monadnock

100

Brattleboro

9

124

Jaffrey

Mass.

New York

Contents

Introduction 6

    Hiking Times and Distances 8

    Getting Started 9

    Hiking Guidelines 10

    Maps 11

Hike Descriptions

  1. Mount Mansfield Region 12

  2. Mt. Hunger and the Worcester Range 26

  3. Camel's Hump 32

  4. Mad River Valley and Mt. Abraham 38

  5. Middlebury and Brandon 44

  6. Killington and Nearby Hikes 50

  7. Mt. Ascutney and Okemo 55

  8. Manchester and Stratton Mountain 60

  9. Bennington Area 66

 10. Mount Snow Area 70

 11. Groton State Forest 75

 12. The Northern Frontier 78

 13. Northeast Kingdom 82

 14. Backcountry Skiing 88

 15. Backpacking on the Long Trail 96

References 103

Index 107

Introduction

Hikers have long enjoyed the hundreds of miles of trails that wind through the mountains of Vermont. The terrain varies from gentle woods paths to rocky scrambles up Vermont's highest peaks. We have tried to make this guide book easy to use by basing the chapters around familiar towns and mountains and then presenting the popular hikes for each recreation area. The detailed maps that accompany the route descriptions show the hiking terrain and the driving approaches to the trailheads. Beginning with the Mt. Mansfield region, our most important hiking area, we present the most commonly done hikes from Camel's Hump, Worcester Range, Mad River Valley, Middlebury, Killington, Manchester, Bennington, Mount Snow, Brattleboro, Ascutney, Groton State Forest, the Northeast Kingdom, and Jay Peak areas. For this second edition, we have added a section on backpacking trips on the Long Trail as well as a concise guide to Vermont's fine backcountry skiing.

Our focus is on mountain hikes, that is, climbing up mountains, usually to the top, but also to a view or something else of interest, say a pond or a cabin. And rather than attempting to provide a list of all trails, or a selection of say, 50 hikes—the two standard approaches for hiking guides—we give a comprehensive selection of complete hikes throughout the state: 95 hikes on 65 mountains. In Vermont, hiking information has traditionally revolved around the Long Trail, the 265-mile "footpath in the wilderness," which runs from Massachusetts to the Canadian border. This has resulted in two guide books: one for the Long Trail system and another guide book for the trails and mountains, which are not connected to the Long Trail. Since both books would then be needed to get adequate coverage of the state, even for day hikes, this turns out to be more costly and less convenient. **Hiker's Guide to the Mountains of Vermont** remedies this by covering perhaps 95% of the mountain hiking activity in one book: the classic hikes, the highest mountains (by most routes), and many local favorites.

Hikers often give themselves long term, or long distance, hiking goals. This usually takes one of two forms: hiking the entire length of a trail like the Appalachian Trail or Long Trail, or climbing all the mountains on an agreed list—such as the 48 mountains over 4,000' in New Hampshire, the 46 over 4,000' in the High Peaks of New York state's Adirondacks, or even all 111 4,000' footers in New England and the Adirondacks combined. While long-distance hiking might be regarded as unimaginative drudgery, and peakbagging an arbitrary pursuit, both goals are great motivators, and encourage hikers to go places and experience things they otherwise would not. As a side note to this discussion it is relevant to point out that Vermont has six mountains over 4,000'—not five as widely believed! If we apply the definitions used in the Adirondacks or in New Hampshire, where peakbagging is practically a sacred endeavor, the 4,062' south summit of Mt. Mansfield—the Nose—qualifies as a separate mountain. This observation is more than a technicality, however. Since a number of important routes to the summit ridge (Haselton Trail, Maple Ridge Trail, Long Trail from the south) terminate at or near the Nose, and the higher summit is over a mile away, it is natural to treat the distinctive south summit as a goal in its own right.

Hiking times and distances

In the mountains, it is walking time rather than distance travelled that can give us a reliable measure of the actual effort needed to do a particular hike. A 3-mile hike in gentle terrain is obviously going to take much less effort than a 3-mile hike up Camel's Hump, which requires almost 3,000' of climbing. In the hike descriptions provided, round trip time, round trip distance, and approximate elevation gained are provided, with the time given first. Actual times will vary a great deal from hiker to hiker, or from day to day depending on trail (and hiker) condition. The times provided are based partly on observation and partly by applying the standard formula of 2 miles per hour plus one half hour per 1,000' gain in elevation. Most hikers should find these time estimates reasonable—some will find them too low, some too high. By providing a *consistent* rating, each hiker should eventually be able to gauge in advance the amount of time he or she will need for a particular hike.

When travelling in the mountains, especially on longer, more ambitious hikes, the main comment about time has to be: Allow yourself plenty! It is up to you to build flexibility into your schedule, so your group has some leeway to deal with unplanned events or delays.

In some areas, trails are showing signs of overuse, and in other areas fragile vegetation is at risk. Please respect any signs—trail detours, or requests not to walk off the trail, for example—that you might encounter. In fact, during the spring mud season, about mid-April to Memorial Day, many of the trails are closed. This is because of the much greater damage done by boots when trails are soft and muddy.

Getting started

Most of the routes in this book will be enjoyable for hikers of all levels of experience, and most can be done at a reasonable pace in half a day, or less. Round trip times and distances are given for each hike, and difficult trail sections are noted in the route descriptions. To get started, begin with the shorter hikes in your area. Find out what sort of footwear you prefer, and get an idea of how *your* normal hiking pace compares with the times given here. You have probably already done some form of hiking or extended walking, and the role of this guide is to encourage you to experience Vermont's most popular hikes.

From the summit of Mount Mansfield

For those who are not comfortable with the do-it-yourself approach, there are also a number of organized hiking tours, and many colleges have outing clubs, as well. In Vermont, the Green Mountain Club is the primary hiking organization. If you are a regular user of hiking trails, consider joining or supporting the GMC or your local hiking club.

Hiking Guidelines

Useful guidelines and reminders:

- Pick a route that is within your group's ability.
- Allow yourself plenty of time.
- Let someone know of your plans, and stick to them.
- Exercise extra caution if hiking alone.
- Pack out what you pack in.
- Pets should be controlled at all times: on a leash near water sources and on summits above treeline.
- Take water with you. The Giardia parasite is unfortunately widespread, so it is best to play it safe.
- Respect owner signs and private property.

Always take extra clothing: preferably something that will keep you dry *and* protect you from wind. Before starting out, consider that there is always a chance the weather will deteriorate during your trip: Be prepared for this. The variability of weather is especially a concern for early summer and fall hikes; even on fine days, mountain summits are usually cooler and breezier than down below.

Since there is such variation in hiking abilities and tastes, our advice on clothing and equipment is to consult your nearest outdoor outfitter. Most of Vermont's hiking/backpacking outfitters are represented in this guide. In part, this recognizes the essential role they play in advising and educating the public about appropriate and cost effective offerings in footwear, waterproof gear, packs, parkas, and accessories. They are a source of local hiking information and current conditions, and several have assisted with the selection of hikes for this guide book.

Maps

Complete topographic map coverage for Vermont, and the rest of the country, is provided by the United States Geological Survey (USGS). There are four different map formats in use. The most widely used format is the 7.5-minute series at a scale of 1:24 000. In a few areas, these have been replaced by the new 1:25 000 metric format (with twice the area). Both formats display information at a very detailed level, and hiking trails are shown. However, some of the 7.5-minute quadrangles were prepared more than 30 years ago.

A 1:100 000 scale metric series (1 degree by 30 minutes) is also available. Although these maps lack the detail of the two series mentioned above, they are very useful in gaining an understanding of a larger area, a county, for example. Major hiking trails are shown, and the contour interval is 20 meters. Both metric map styles come folded, with a cover, as opposed to the loose sheet style of the non-metric series.

The 15-minute series (1:62 500) has been discontinued by the USGS. This is regrettable, as the scale is a good compromise between the need for detail and the desire to see the larger area, and they are perhaps the most successful of the USGS maps in "bringing the terrain to life".

The Vermont Atlas and Gazetteer (DeLorme) and *Vermont Road and Atlas Guide* (Northern Cartographic) are useful in navigating back roads and finding trailheads; they are valuable for their excellent level of detail. See the appendix for information on other maps and map suppliers.

Mount Mansfield 4,393'

As the highest mountain in Vermont, and the dominant landmark in the Burlington area, Mount Mansfield naturally receives a great deal of attention from hikers. The Long Trail traverses its 2-mile, open summit ridge, and there are nine hiking routes up the mountain. A gondola and a toll road to the summit ridge make the upper mountain accessible to everyone. The following pages describe the main routes up Mount Mansfield, as well as some nearby hikes: Sterling Pond, Elephant's Head, and Whiteface Mountain. Two areas to the south, Nebraska Notch and Bolton Valley, are also discussed as part of the Mount Mansfield region.

Long Trail route up Mt. Mansfield

The popular route from the Stowe side follows the Long Trail south (actually west) from Route 108. This excellent trail climbs steadily and steeply through woods, reaching **Taft Lodge** (caretaker in summer) after 1.7 miles and about 1.5 hours. From here, the trail is rougher and steeper, breaking into the open about 10 minutes past Taft. The exciting final section to the summit is up steep rocks. Although it is not really difficult, use caution, especially if the rocks are wet. The 360-degree view from the summit is spectacular. Return by the same route, or, for a route more protected from the elements, continue south from the summit on the LT (for 0.2 mile) and turn left on the **Profanity Trail**. It uses a steep gully to descend to Taft Lodge and the Long Trail.

5 hours and 4.7 miles round trip. Elevation gain: 2,800'
Approach: From Stowe, drive west on Rt. 108 for 8.5 miles, passing the ski area entrances, and park at the Long Trail.

The Chin from the north

Hell Brook Trail

One of the most continuously steep and rough trails in Vermont, Hell Brook is not recommended for beginners. However, many experienced hikers (and expert powder skiers) will want to do this challenging trail. Not advised for the descent, and especially not when it is raining! After its long, arduous climb, the trail breaks into the open upon reaching the summit ridge, about 1.3 miles from the road. (**Hell Brook Cut-off Trail** branches left to **Taft Lodge** at 0.9 mile.) Head left to reach the Long Trail, and follow it to the summit—only 1.8 miles from the road. The recommended descent route is via the **Long Trail** and Taft Lodge, leaving you with an easy 1-mile road walk back to your car.

The Toll Road up Mount Mansfield

Starting from the Toll House on the Mountain Road, 6 miles from Stowe, the gravel-surfaced Toll Road climbs to the summit ridge of Mount Mansfield in 4.5 miles. From here, it is an easy, and spectacular 1.4-mile hike north along the Long Trail to the **Chin**, the summit of Mount Mansfield. Presumably most drive up the Toll Road, but it is open to hikers at no charge. Once on the summit ridge, hikers must stay on the actual trail (or rock outcroppings) as the fragile arctic vegetation is easily damaged by foot traffic. The **Nose** (4,062'), the mountain's southern summit, looms just above the parking area, and a short hike (20 minutes) brings you to the top. There are excellent views of the summit ridge for many miles in all directions. Guide books and maps can be purchased at the **Summit Station**, located at the top of the Toll Road.

Looking north along the summit ridge to the Chin

The Gondola and the Cliff Trail

Another relatively expedient way up Mt. Mansfield is to ride the ski area's gondola, and then hike the remaining 0.7 mile to the summit. The gondola ends a few hundred feet below the summit ridge, and once the summit ridge is reached, it is an easy walk to the top. The problem is getting to the ridge; the **Cliff Trail** is quite difficult in a few places and involves brief climbing up and over some large boulders. Head right (south) 150' from the gondola to pick up the Cliff Trail. Once on the ridge, head right (north) on the **Long Trail** for the remaining 15 minutes (0.4 mile) to the top. Note this trail junction for your return. An easier and longer descent route is as follows: From the top, head down the Long Trail the way you came, but stay on the beautiful, open summit ridge (1.4 miles) to the **Toll Road**. Then head down the Toll Road, and turn left onto the first ski run, the **Nosedive**. Follow this and other ski runs down the mountain, returning to the gondola base station and completing the loop.

3–4 hours and 4 miles total. (Descend via ski trails.)

Approach: The base station of the gondola is 7.5 miles from Route 100 in Stowe, on Route 108 (the Mountain Road).

The Nose (4,062') via the Haselton Trail

Angling up to the left from the base of the gondola (approach as above), the Haselton Trail climbs at a pleasant angle, crossing several ski trails, before merging with **Nosedive** (ski run) and ending on the **Toll Road** (at 1.6 miles) just below the Octagon restaurant. Follow the Toll Road (right) 0.5 mile to the **Summit House** on the summit ridge. From here a short scramble (0.2 mile) on the **Triangle Trail** leads to the top of the impressive probiscus. Descend by the same route.

3–4 hours, 4.6 miles total. Elevation gain: 2,500'

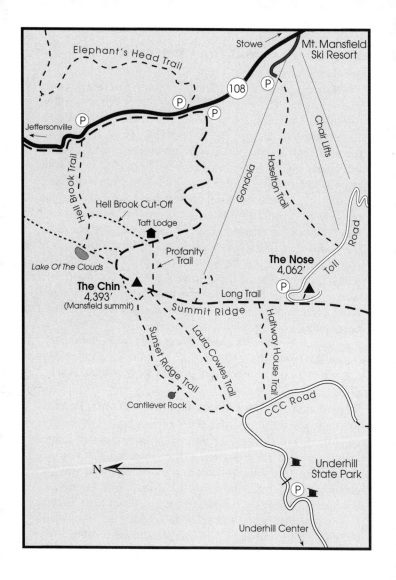

16 Mount Mansfield

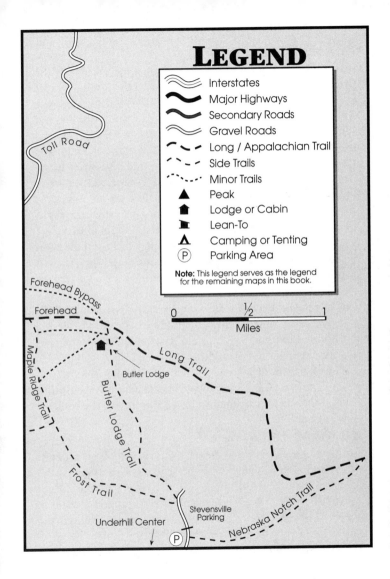

LEGEND

≈	Interstates
≈	Major Highways
≈	Secondary Roads
≈	Gravel Roads
– –	Long / Appalachian Trail
– –	Side Trails
⋯	Minor Trails
▲	Peak
⬠	Lodge or Cabin
▮	Lean-To
⩜	Camping or Tenting
Ⓟ	Parking Area

Note: This legend serves as the legend for the remaining maps in this book.

0   ½   1
Miles

Toll Road

Forehead Bypass

Forehead

Maple Ridge Trail

Butler Lodge

Long Trail

Butler Lodge Trail

Frost Trail

Stevensville Parking

Underhill Center

Ⓟ

Nebraska Notch Trail

Sunset Ridge Trail

On the west side of Mount Mansfield, Sunset Ridge is the prominent ridge dropping off the summit. Because of its spectacular views of the Champlain Valley and the Adirondacks, this popular route is one of the finest hikes in Vermont. From Underhill State Park (nominal fee), ascend the **CCC Road** for about a mile, where the Sunset Ridge and Laura Cowles Trails branch left. Continue on Sunset Ridge Trail as it climbs steeply through woods, eventually coming out on the broad, open ridge. From here to the **Chin** (the summit) the route is out in the open, and the sweeping views to the west of the Adirondacks and Lake Champlain are impressive, especially in late afternoon. The low-angle slabs make for generally easy hiking. On the summit ridge, bear left (north) on the **Long Trail** to the summit, 0.2 mile farther on. Descend by the same route.

5 hours and 6.6 miles round trip. Elevation gain: 2,550'
Approach: From Underhill (on Route 15), drive to Underhill Center. Continue to Mountain Road, a short distance beyond, and take it to Underhill State Park.
Side trail: About 0.7 mile above the CCC Road, a short (0.1-mile) spur trail leads left to well-known **Cantilever Rock**, a rock that juts horizontally about 25' out over the trail.

Halfway House Trail

South of Laura Cowles, the Halfway House Trail ascends Mansfield's west flank, with better views than the Laura Cowles Trail. Leave the CCC Rd. 0.2 mile past the Sunset Ridge turn off, and reach the summit ridge after 1.1 miles of steep climbing. Head left on the Long Trail for 1.2 miles to the top. The normal descent route is down the Sunset Ridge.

5–6 hours and 6.8 miles round trip. A 2,550' climb.

Sunset Ridge from Maple Ridge

Laura Cowles Trail

From Underhill State Park, walk up the CCC Road. After about a mile, the Laura Cowles and Sunset Ridge trails branch left off the road, and after 0.1 mile, Laura Cowles Trail branches right. This trail ascends very directly to the summit ridge, at times climbing stone stairs. It rejoins the Sunset Ridge Trail just west of the Long Trail. The views are limited until near the top. Take the Long Trail for 0.2 mile to the summit. The best descent route is via the open Sunset Ridge, thus you "walk into the view" as you hike down.

Maps: *USGS Mt. Mansfield 1:100 000 (metric),*
USGS Mt. Mansfield 1:24 000,
Trail Map of Mt. Mansfield (GMC), and
Hiker's Guide to Mt. Mansfield.

Maple Ridge

Sunset Ridge and Maple Ridge are the two main west ridges of Mount Mansfield. Maple Ridge descends from the Forehead towards Underhill Center. From the parking lot at the end of Stevensville Rd., take the **Frost Trail** to **Maple Ridge Trail**. Continue up the ridge (it changes to **Wampahoofus Trail**) to the **Forehead's** open summit at 3,940'. This route has some rather difficult sections, but it is absolutely one of the most exciting trails in Vermont! The views constantly change as the trail works its way across huge slabs and around improbable rock formations. From the Forehead, either descend the Long Trail (south), or continue (north on the LT) to the Nose, or the Chin, depending on time, weather, etc. To descend from the Forehead, follow the Long Trail south, passing several ladders. After 0.8 mile, branch right to **Butler Lodge**, and continue down to the Stevensville parking area.

Maple Ridge-Forehead-Butler Lodge loop:
5 hours and 5 miles round trip. Elevation gain: 2,550'
The Nose is 0.8 mile farther, the Chin, 2 miles.
Approach: From Underhill Center, drive to the end of Stevensville Road and park. Walk up the (gated) road, taking the Frost Trail (left) 0.2 mile from the car.

Forehead Bypass

As an easier variation on the above, hike to Butler Lodge from Stevensville, then via the Long Trail to the Forehead. The Nose is about 30 minutes farther. On the descent, use the weather-protected Forehead Bypass (east of the LT), an easier, pleasant route through a cool and mossy birch wood. After rejoining the LT, retrace your path to Butler Lodge and continue down to the parking at Stevensville.

5 hours and 5.5 miles round trip. Elevation gain: 2,550'

Long Trail to Sterling Pond

This extremely popular hike leads to a pleasant mountain pond and, a short distance away, a sweeping view north from the top of a ski run. From **Smugglers Notch** (2,612), take the well-maintained Long Trail north as it climbs fairly steeply and steadily. Bear left at the pond for a short distance to reach the ski area viewpoint. Sterling Pond Shelter and Watson Camp are 0.3 mile farther on. Descend by the same route. (See Elephant's Head Trail)

2 hours, 2.2 miles round trip. Elevation gain: 930'

Approach: Park at (the top of) Smugglers Notch on Route 108, 10 miles from Stowe and 8 miles from Jeffersonville.

Elephant's Head

This difficult and varied hike leads to a spectacular ledge 1,000' above Smugglers Notch. From the south end of the picnic area, cross the stream, then ascend very steeply (for 20 min.), soon crossing a landslide ravine (good views). From here, the trail is intermittently quite rough. It skirts the edge of the steep mountainside (a cliff), but the dense forest gives a feeling of security, while only partially obscuring the dramatic views of Mansfield. A spur trail (0.1 mile) descends very steeply to dramatic Elephant's Head ledge. *Note:* The spur trail might be closed during the summer months to protect Peregrine Falcon nesting. Return by the same route, or continue to Sterling Pond and on down to Smugglers Notch via the Long Trail (longer).

3 hours and 4.4 miles (up and back). Elevation gain: 1,500'

Approach: Park at the Smugglers Notch picnic area on Route 108, above the entrances to the Stowe ski area—on the right, a short distance beyond the Long Trail sign.

Whiteface Mountain 3,715'

The pointed summit of this steep-sided peak has good views through and around the trees. From the car, walk in on a woods road for 2 miles (blue blazes) to where the **Whiteface Mountain Trail** turns off to the right. It then climbs steadily, reaching **Whiteface Shelter** and the Long Trail after a mile. Bear right 0.4 mile on the LT, which climbs steeply to the summit. Descend by the same route, or, for a good loop hike, continue south on the Long Trail past the Whiteface Trail junction, over **Morse Mountain**, past **Hagerman Lookout** to **Chilcoot Pass**, in the saddle below **Madonna Mountain** (Smugglers Notch Ski Area). From here, head left and descend extremely steeply for 0.8 mile to **Beaver Meadow Lodge**, then keep left to return to the road used on the way in.

> *Loop: 5 hours and 8.7 miles. Total elevation gain: 2,400'*
> *Approach:* From Morristown Corners (north of Stowe), head west on Walton Rd., then *south* on Cole Hill Rd. At 2 miles, turn right on Mud City Rd. At 4.4 miles, turn left on Beaver Meadow Rd. Park in the clearing at 5.8 miles.

Nebraska Notch 1,850'

From the private Lake Mansfield Trout Club, hike along the lake, then up a steep section to **Taylor Lodge** and the **Long Trail**, where there are views over Nebraska Valley. Return by the same route. From Nebraska Notch, it is 6 miles on the Long Trail (past Dewey Mtn.) to the top of Mount Mansfield.

> *2.5 hours and 3 miles round trip. Elevation gain: 750'*
> *Approach:* From Route 100, just south of Stowe, drive through Moscow to the end of Nebraska Valley.
> *Bushwhack hike:* There is no trail up steep, densely forested **Dewey Mountain** (3,330'). Seen from the east or from the Forehead on Mansfield, it is an intriguing mountain.

Ricker Mountain 3,401' (Bolton Valley)

From the ski area base lodge, ascend the ski slopes under the Number 2 chairlift, then follow the service road to the top of Number 4 chair. From here, continuing the line of the lift, find the path that leads to the wooden observation tower. The views are excellent, especially of Camel's Hump. Descend by the same route.

2 hours and 2 miles round trip. Elevation gain: 1,400'
Approach: Drive to the Bolton Valley Ski Area. The 4-mile access road leaves Route 2, 6 miles west of Waterbury. From Burlington, use the Richmond exit off I-89 and Rt. 2.

Bolton Mountain 3,725'

The isolated, rounded shape of this relatively high but view-less mountain is a prominent part of the landscape as seen from I-89 and Burlington. From Bolton's ski touring center, hike up the George's Gorge and Ravens Wind ski trails, eventually reaching the Long Trail. Continue (right) for about 0.7 mile to the top. Descend by the same route.

About 4 hours round trip.

Harrington's View 2,520'

For a shorter, and probably more interesting hike than the above, start from the Ski Touring Center, and walk out Broadway to Bobcat. At the top of Bobcat, continue to Eagle's Nest, and from there, hike up to the Long Trail. Harrington's View, an open rock ledge with a nice view, is then about 20 minutes to the south (left). Return on the same trails.

2 hours, 3 miles, elevation gain: 500'
Approach: As above, drive to Bolton Valley Ski Area.
Map: Free area map is available at the Bolton Valley store.

The Worcester Range

The impressive mountain wall that parallels Route 100 from Waterbury past Stowe to Morrisville is known as the Worcester Range. High above Waterbury Center, popular Mount Hunger is the bare, rounded knoll on the ridge—just to the right of a slightly higher point on the ridge. The Skyline Ridge Trail runs along this ridge from Mount Hunger to Hogback Mountain and eventually down into Stowe Hollow.

Mt. Hunger 3,538'

This classic hike affords some of the best mountaintop views in Vermont: Camel's Hump looms to the south, Waterbury Reservoir is below, and Mt. Mansfield beckons to the northwest. The White Mountains of New Hampshire are visible on a clear day. From the parking area, the **Waterbury Trail** ascends through woods, gradually at first, then steadily and steeply in its upper section—at times clambering up giant "steps". The trail breaks into the open just below the top. Be sure to note your surroundings as you enter the open summit area, in order to find the trail back down easily. There are two other trails off the summit and no signs. Mount Hunger is known for its blueberries in July and August.

4 hours, 3.8 miles round trip. Elev. gain: 2,290'
Approach: From Waterbury Center, just east of Route 100, drive north on Maple Street, then right on Loomis Hill Road. Stay left at 2.7 miles, park at 3.7 miles.

Just below the summit of Mt. Hunger, the trail to **White Rock Mtn.** (3,194') branches right. This rough trail leads to the interesting open rocks on White Rock Mtn., including a huge, level rock slab below the summit. The trail then heads around to the east side of the ridge and ends on the **Middlesex Trail**, about a mile below the top of Mt. Hunger. This is a longer way to do Mt. Hunger, offering an interesting, fun variation.

Skyline Ridge Trail

This relatively new and as yet little-used trail seems to be slowly gaining acceptance. To do the complete traverse, climb Mount Hunger from the Waterbury Center side (This is more convenient for car shuttling than from Middlesex). From the summit, head left (north), and follow the blue-blazed trail as it works its way along the ridge over the north summit of Hunger and on to Hogback. There are occasional outlooks with good views. After about 2 miles, the trail descends steeply to **Stowe Pinnacle** and Stowe Hollow. At the Pinnacle Trail, it is only 0.2 mile (left) to the wide-open top of Stowe Pinnacle (very worthwhile for the dramatic views), and 1.3 miles down to the road in Stowe Hollow. This challenging hike, over steep and rough terrain, is an interesting alternative to many of our more heavily used trails.

5–7 hours and 7 miles (one way). Elevation gain: 2,900'
Approach: Same as for the trail up Mount Hunger from Waterbury Center, via Loomis Hill Road.
Future plans: Plans are in place to continue the Skyline Ridge Trail north to Mt. Elmore—during the summer of 1996, crews plan to clear as far north as Mt. Worcester.

Maps: *USGS 1:100 000 Mount Mansfield (metric),*
         USGS 1:24 000 Stowe, Morrisville, Mt. Worcester,
         Summer Recreation Map & Guide to the
         Mount Mansfield Region, and
         Hiker's Guide to Mount Mansfield.

Mount Hunger from Middlesex

Somewhat longer than the Waterbury route, this trail is the standard route for folks approaching from Montpelier. It is a more varied trail, and the upper section negotiates a series of interesting slabs. Not recommended when icy! The signage leaves something to be desired, but the blue-blazed trail is excellent and recommended as a change for those who usually climb Mount Hunger from the Waterbury side. (After 1.5 miles, the **White Rock Trail** branches to the left.) Because there are two other trails, note the route carefully as you approach the summit to avoid confusion on your descent.

4 hours and 5.6 miles round trip. Elevation gain: 1,900'
Approach: From Montpelier, drive north on Route 12 to Shady Rill Road and turn left. After 2.2 miles, turn right on Worcester Road for 0.7 mile, then left for 1.8 miles to a clearing and the parking area.

Stowe Pinnacle 2,740'

This very popular, moderately strenuous hike starts out as a gentle climb (usually somewhat muddy), before gradually getting steeper and rockier. The trail levels off in a saddle (there is a spur trail left to a lookout), then descends steeply a short way before climbing to the spectacular open summit. Stay right at the (possibly unmarked) junction of the **Skyline Ridge Trail** (to Mount Hunger and Waterbury) about 0.2 mile below the top. From the broad, open summit, there is a superb view across Stowe to Mount Mansfield. The view extends from Camel's Hump in the south to Jay Peak in the north, with the Worcester Range directly above.

2.5–3 hours and 3 miles round trip. Elevation gain: 1,520'
Approach: From Stowe, drive to Stowe Hollow, and follow Upper Hollow Road to a small parking lot on the left.

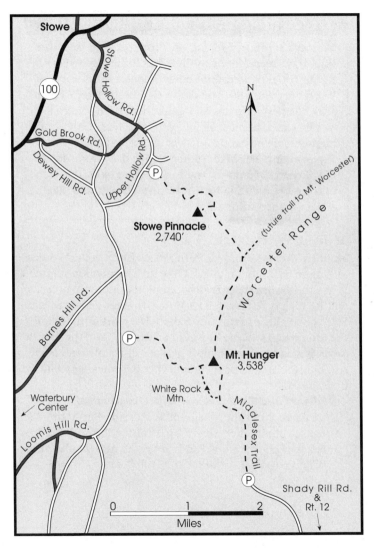

Stowe

100

Stowe Hollow Rd.

Gold Brook Rd.

Dewey Hill Rd.

Upper Hollow Rd.

N

P

Stowe Pinnacle
2,740'

(future trail to Mt. Worcester)

Worcester Range

Barnes Hill Rd.

P

Mt. Hunger
3,538'

White Rock
Mtn.

Middlesex Trail

Waterbury
Center

Loomis Hill Rd.

P

Shady Rill Rd.
&
Rt. 12

0   1   2
Miles

Worcester Range 29

Green Mountain Club's Hiker Center

Vermont's primary hiking and backpacking organization, the Green Mountain Club, has its headquarters on Route 100 in Waterbury Center, about 4 miles north of Waterbury and I-89. The club's Gameroff Hiker Center sells a variety of maps and guide books, and there are displays and photos of interest to hikers. GMC staff members are on hand to answer questions and help with trip planning. The hiker center is open daily from Memorial Day to Columbus Day. In the off-season, the club office is open during regular business hours, and hikers are always welcome.

Mount Worcester 3,293'

Mount Worcester is probably the least visited of the Worcester Range peaks, but it offers a fine hike to an open summit. When the **Skyline Ridge Trail** is completed, Mount Worcester will be connected by trail to Mount Hunger and to Stowe. Perhaps it will see more visitors then. The existing trail climbs the mountain from the Worcester side, i.e. from the east. It ascends steadily, for the most part at quite a pleasant angle, reaching the broad, rocky summit after 2.5 miles. Descend by the same trail.

3.5 hours and 5 miles round trip. Elevation gain: 1,970'

Approach: From the village of Worcester (on Route 12, north of Montpelier), drive up Minister Brook Road 1.5 miles to Hampshire Road and turn right. At 3.9 miles, turn left, and park at 4.1 miles.

Mount Elmore 2,608'

Although it is the lowest of the Worcester Range peaks described here, Mount Elmore is immediately noticed from most vantage points in the Stowe-Morrisville area because of its isolated position at the end of the ridge. It is very prominent from the Trapp Family Lodge, for example. Climb the tower on the summit for great views of the lake, nearby farms, Mount Mansfield, and the mountains to the north such as Belvidere and Mount Pisgah. From the state park, follow the blue-blazed trail (it starts out as a service road) for about 2 miles to the open summit. Descend by the same route. Near the top, a half-mile spur trail leads to **Balanced Rock**.

2.5 hours and 4.2 miles round trip. Elevation gain: 1,450'
Approach: From Morrisville, drive north 4 miles on Route 12 to Lake Elmore State Park. There is a nominal day use fee.

Camel's Hump 4,083'

One of Vermont's best known landmarks, Camel's Hump offers possibly the finest mountaintop in the state. Unspoiled by roads, ski areas, and communication antennas, its compact, rocky summit floats high above Burlington and the Champlain Valley. The Adirondacks are 50 miles to the west across Lake Champlain; the White Mountains of New Hampshire define the eastern horizon; and the Green Mountain chain stretches to the north and south.

From the west: the Burrows Trail

This popular route from Huntington climbs moderately at first, but with increasing steepness, slackening shortly before intersecting the Long Trail (2.1 miles) at a small clearing, 0.3 mile from the top. From the clearing, turn right onto the Long Trail and scramble up the steep and rocky trail, coming out into the open shortly before the summit. Descend by the same route or by a variation, as described below.

4 hours and 4.8 miles round trip. Elevation gain: 1,950'

Approach: From Richmond (exit 11 on I-89), drive south 9 miles through Huntington to Huntington Center. Turn left on Camel's Hump Road, and follow it 3.5 miles to the end.

Forest City Trail variation: Immediately after starting out on the Burrows Trail, turn right onto the short connector trail to the Forest City Trail. Here head left, and climb up to **Wind Gap** on the LT at 1.4 miles. Montclair Glen Lodge is just to the right, and the top is north (left) along a demanding and very interesting 2-mile section of the LT. The final climb out in the open, around the mountain's south face, is spectacular. Descend by the Burrows. A classic route.

About 5 hours and 6 miles round trip.

Camel's Hump from Huntington

From the east: the Forestry Trail

Probably the most popular route up Camel's Hump, the Forestry Trail is the natural route for those coming from Stowe or Montpelier. A wide, comfortable trail, especially in the first mile, it passes the **Dean Trail** at 1.3 miles and higher up, crosses the **Alpine Trail** at 2.5 miles. (The Alpine Trail traverses the east flank of the mountain, from near Gorham Lodge to a point on the LT at the base of the cliffs on the mountain's south side.) After 3.1 miles, the Forestry Trail ends on the LT, at the clearing just north of the summit. The Burrows Trail, approaching from the west, ends here also. Now head south (left) for 0.3 mile over steep and rocky terrain to conclude the climb. Descend by the same route or by the Dean Trail variation. (See the next page.)

4 hours and 6.8 miles round trip. Elevation gain: 1,800'

Approach: From Waterbury (I-89, exit 10), take Rt. 2 through Waterbury, turn right on Rt. 100, and then immediately right again onto River Rd. Follow it 4 miles, then turn left and continue (climbing) for 3.5 miles to the parking area.

Camel's Hump 33

Variation on Forestry Trail: 1.3 miles up the Forestry Trail, the **Dean Trail** branches left to **Wind Gap** and the Long Trail. From Wind Gap, head right on the LT for 1.7 miles to the top. The trail is quite steep and rough just above Wind Gap, followed by an easy section, before a prolonged steep climb up to the base of the final cliffs, which are skirted to the left. (The remains of a 1940s plane wreck can be seen a short way down the **Alpine Trail**.) The final climb up the low angle summit slabs makes for a great finish. Descend north on the LT, turning (right) down the Forestry Trail, 0.3 mile below the top. This loop is a fine way to do the mountain from the east.

About 5 hours, 7.5 miles. Elevation gain: 1,800'

Bamforth Ridge Trail

Although it receives a fraction of the traffic of the Burrows and Forestry Trails, the Bamforth Ridge Trail is in excellent condition. Starting at an elevation of only 350', it climbs steadily, at times quite steeply, to gain the top of the steep northern end of Bamforth Ridge. After about 1.5 hours, you reach the first of several open, ledgy sections with good views of the Hump and vistas to the east and west. From here, the trail takes on a more undulating character, crossing numerous open areas with good views. The final stiff climb of over 1,000' takes you past the **Alpine Trail** to the Long Trail at **Gorham Lodge** (3,400') and onto the summit, 0.9 mile beyond Gorham Lodge. Descend by the same route, or by one of the other trails. See the Long Trail variation below.

7–8 hours, 11.8 miles round trip. Elevation gain: 4,000'
Approach: Cross the Jonesville bridge (Route 2, east of Richmond) and drive east (left) on River Road for 3.5 miles (past the Long Trail) to the small parking area on the left.

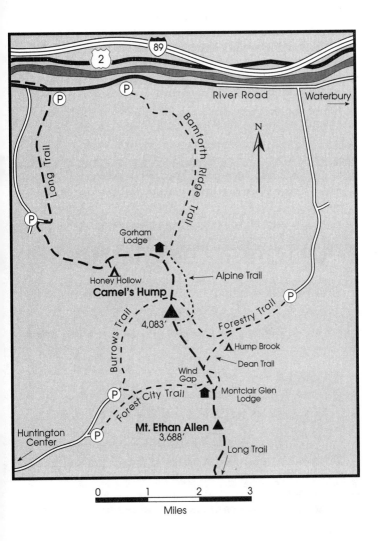

89

2

River Road

Waterbury

P

P

N

Long Trail

Bamforth Ridge Trail

P

Gorham Lodge

Alpine Trail

Honey Hollow

Camel's Hump

Forestry Trail

P

Burrows Trail

4,083'

Hump Brook

Dean Trail

Wind Gap

P

Forest City Trail

Montclair Glen Lodge

Huntington Center

P

Mt. Ethan Allen
3,688'

Long Trail

0   1   2   3
Miles

***Long Trail variation on the Bamforth Ridge
route:*** On the descent, at **Gorham Lodge**, stay (left) on the
Long Trail, following it down to River Road. The interesting
upper section runs along a narrow ridge, before dropping
steeply to a pleasant woods road. Head right on **River Road**
for about a mile to return to the Bamforth Ridge trailhead.
It is 5.5 miles from Gorham Lodge to River Road. The total
loop distance, including the road section, is about 14 miles.

Maps: *USGS Camel's Hump 1:24 000,
USGS Mt. Mansfield 1:100 000 (metric),* and
Hiker's Guide to Mount Mansfield.

Winter activity on Camel's Hump

In recent winters, hikers and backcountry skiers have been very active on the mountain. The Burrows, Forestry, Forest City, and Dean trails all seem to receive regular attention from skiers and snowshoers. It is frequently possible to hike pleasantly on a packed trail to the top of Camel's Hump in the middle of winter. Telemarkers enjoy the steep slopes on the east side of the mountain, especially off the Alpine Trail. The Forestry/Dean Trail route to the beaver pond below Wind Gap is a favorite among snowshoers.

Coming from the south, the **Catamount Ski Trail** traverses the west side of the mountain at a low elevation (1,500') before descending north-facing **Honey Hollow** to meet the Long Trail for the final section down to River Road in Jonesville. For more information on skiing, see the backcountry skiing chapter starting on page 88.

The mountains in winter

Outdoor winter activity in northern New England, especially at higher elevations or in remote locations, requires a greater level of preparation and conditioning than trips over the same terrain in the summer. There are various factors to consider: The days are much shorter (i.e. early darkness), there is a potential for rapid deterioration in conditions (drop in temperature, strong winds, reduced visibility, changing snow conditions), and it is generally more difficult to find and follow trails in winter. Perhaps the most surprising difference between summer and winter is the extreme variability of conditions ... what was easy and fun last week, or just an hour ago, can turn into a very serious undertaking.

The Mad River Valley

Home of the Sugarbush and Mad River Glen ski areas, the "Valley" offers good hiking, including two or three classic trips. In particular, the section of the Long Trail between Lincoln Gap and Appalachian Gap is something most hikers will want to do. This narrow, 11-mile ridge includes Mount Abraham, Mount Ellen, and the tops of the three ski areas. Waitsfield and Warren are the two towns in the valley.

Mount Abraham 4,006'

The lowest of Vermont's five mountains over 4,000', Mt. Abraham just barely pokes above the treeline. It is a great trip for kids who are up for 4 to 5 hours of hiking. From Lincoln Gap, follow the Long Trail north over varied terrain, passing **Battell Shelter** at 1.7 miles (The Battell Trail comes in from the left), and reaching the summit at 2.6 miles. The final section of the trail is steeper in spots and involves a little easy scrambling up large rock slabs. The superb view is known for giving a sensation of peering straight down on the farms of Lincoln. This is a fantastic spot during fall foliage.

4 hours and 5.2 miles round trip. Elevation gain: 1,700'
Approach: From Warren, drive up Lincoln Gap Road, and park in one of the parking lots just below the top.

Sunset Ledge

This short, out-and-back hike south on the Long Trail from Lincoln Gap is about 40 minutes of walking each way. The ledges are just off the trail to the right. A dramatic spot with great views of Lincoln, and in the distance, the Adirondacks.

1.5 hours and 2 miles round trip.
Approach: Drive to Lincoln Gap from Warren or Lincoln.

Mount Abraham from Lincoln

Mount Abraham via the Battell Trail

The route up Mount Abraham from the Lincoln side is somewhat longer and involves more climbing than from Lincoln Gap, elevation 2,410'. The trail climbs moderately over its 2-mile length, and ends on the Long Trail, just south of **Battell Shelter**. From here, continue north on the Long Trail to the summit. The trail breaks into the open just below the top. Return by the same trail. The arctic grasses and other vegetation that grow at the summit area are easily damaged by foot traffic and regenerate very slowly. Therefore, hikers are asked to keep off the grass!

5 hours and 5.8 miles round trip. Elevation gain: 2,550'

Approach: From Lincoln, drive north on Quaker St. for 0.5 mile, turning right on Elder Rd. Follow signs to trailhead.

Lincoln Gap to Appalachian Gap

Between these two gaps, the crest of the Green Mountains forms a narrow, well-defined ridge that keeps a high elevation. From Lincoln Gap, take the Long Trail north past Battell Shelter to the summit of **Mt. Abraham** (2 hours). From here, it is 2 miles to the top of **Sugarbush Ski Area** (Castlerock lift). Continuing along the narrow and heavily forested ridge, cross the top of **Mount Ellen** (excellent views) and **Sugarbush North Ski Area** after 4 hours of walking and 6.5 miles. (If it is necessary to cut the trip short, descend to the base of the ski area.) After descending from Ellen, pass the **Jerusalem Trail** on the left, and at 8 miles, the short spur trail (right) to **Glen Ellen Lodge**. A mile farther on, you reach the top of **Mad River Glen** and **Stark's Nest**, from which there are good views. From here it is 2.5 miles on to Route 17 in Appalachian Gap.

7–8 hours, 11.6 miles. Elevation gain northbound: 2,520'
Approach: Start from Lincoln Gap or Appalachian Gap. Appalachian Gap is on Route 17, 6 miles west of Waitsfield. See the Long Trail chapter, page 96, for other LT trips.

Jerusalem Trail up Mt. Ellen (4,083')

This is a fine west-side approach, similar to the Battell Trail on Mt. Abraham. From the car, follow the trail for 2.5 miles to the ridge and the Long Trail. The trail is gentle in its lower section, then steepens as it nears the Long Trail. From here it is 1.8 miles (right) to the top of Mt. Ellen, and the 0.2-mile spur trail to **Glen Ellen Lodge** is just to the north. It is 1.7 miles north to the top of the single chairlift at Mad River Glen (good views).

5–6 hours and 8.6 miles round trip. Elevation gain: 2,580'
Approach: From Rt. 116, drive 3.3 miles up Route 17 and bear right on Jerusalem Rd., then left on Jim Dwire Rd. at 4.6 miles. The trailhead is on the right after 0.5 mile.

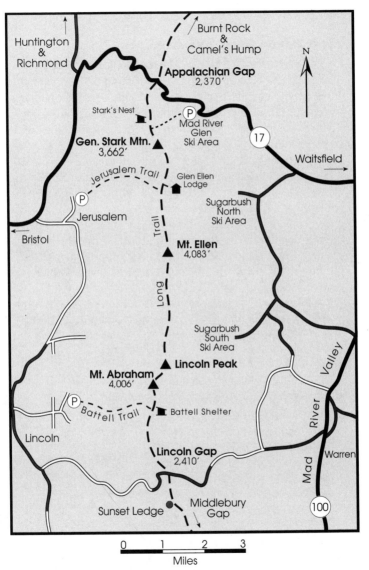

Mad River Glen Ski Area and
General Stark Mountain (3,662')

The goal here is to climb up the ski runs to the top of Mad River Glen's legendary single chairlift. This is the lift on your left, as seen from the base of the ski area. There are only a few lifts, so it is possible to hike out of sight of cables and lift towers. There are beautiful large maples and birches, and the woods are well-groomed, creating the effect of a steep park. At the top of the lift (3,644'), there is an abandoned building (**Stark's Nest**), with a deck that is a good place to relax and enjoy the view. Mad River's runs are very steep, and there are occasional cliffs, thus it is a good idea to take it easy when descending. Take the ski run just south of the top when starting down. General Stark Mountain is a short (0.6 mile, 20 minutes) walk south on the Long Trail and is slightly higher than Stark's Nest.

3–4 hours and 3–4 miles round trip. Elevation gain: 2,000'
Approach: From Waitsfield, drive west on Route 17 to the large parking area at the base of Mad River Glen.

Maps: *USGS 1:24 000 Lincoln, Mt. Ellen, Waitsfield, USGS Montpelier 1:100 000 (metric),* and *Summer Recreation Map & Guide for the Mad River Valley.*

Is the Water Safe To Drink?

When you are hot and thirsty, it's hard to resist a sparkling brook. Used to be you could safely drink water from streams and rivulets. But today, with the Giardia lamlia parasite—a widespread microscopic organism—the recommendation is to boil all drinking water for about five minutes. If filtering, be sure to have the correct kind of filter. Iodine and chlorine treatments are poor options, as they don't destroy the parasite.

The symptoms are nasty: diarrhea, gas, stomach cramps, weight loss, and nausea. In some cases, the symptoms can be with you for months, so this isn't something to take lightly! Animals and people pass the parasite through feces, thus the rule of burying waste at least 200' from any water source.

Middlebury and Brandon

The hikes for this area are spread around: Snake Mountain rises out of the farming country west of Middlebury; Rattlesnake Point is high above Lake Dunmore; Mt. Horrid Overlook is in Brandon Gap; and the Robert Frost Lookout is reached by hiking through Middlebury College's Snow Bowl Ski Area. And, last, we give various hikes that use the Long Trail between Middlebury Gap and South Lincoln.

Snake Mountain 1,287'

Snake Mountain is a distinctive north-south running ridge of hills that rises almost 1,000' above the farms of Addison County. The views of Lake Champlain and the Adirondacks from the top of the cliffs are beautiful, especially in the late afternoon. From the gate, walk up the pleasant woods road. After a "T" (head left), the route steepens and zig-zags up the mountainside. Once you are on the ridge, watch for the side trail (left) out onto the top of the cliffs, where there is an old foundation. You might see ravens gliding above the line of cliffs. Return by the same route.

2.5 hours and 3.6 miles round trip. Elevation gain: 950'
Approach: From Middlebury, take Rt. 125 to Rt. 22A—then drive north for 4.5 miles to Wilmarth Road. Turn right and continue to Mountain Road and a gated woods road.

Maps: *USGS 1:24 000 E. Middlebury, Breadloaf, Lincoln,*
            USGS 1:100 000 Rutland (metric),
            Moosalamoo Partnership's Map (topographic),
            USFS Green Mtn. Nat. Forest, Northern Half, and
            Recreation Map and Guide to Addison County.

Emily Proctor-Cooley Glen Loop

A solid day's hike, this loop is formed by two access trails to the Long Trail and the connecting 5.6-mile section along the trail itself. Although the route is almost entirely wooded, there is a fine, open ledge near the top of Mount Roosevelt called **Killington Overlook**. From the trailhead, take the trail to **Cooley Glen Shelter**, reaching the LT after 3.4 miles. Turn right, heading south along the LT, passing Killington Overlook at 7 miles, and reaching **Emily Proctor Shelter** at 9 miles. From here, it is 3.5 miles down the Emily Proctor Trail to your starting point. The mountains traversed on this section of the Long Trail are: Mt. Cleveland, Mt. Roosevelt, and Mt. Wilson (at 3,745', the highest).

7–8 hours, 12.5 mile loop. Elevation gain: 3,120'

Approach: From Lincoln (east of Bristol), drive through South Lincoln to Forest Road #201 (USFS signs). Turn left and proceed to the trailhead and parking.

Variations:

To climb **Breadloaf Mountain** (3,835'), hike to Emily Proctor Shelter, then south on the LT for 0.7 mile. A short spur trail to the west leads to good views from this summit, the highest between Lincoln and Middlebury Gaps. (For a shorter route to Breadloaf (7 miles round trip), see the trail description to **Skylight Pond**.)

To climb **Mt. Grant** (3,623'), take the Cooley Glen Trail, and at the LT head left (north) for 0.8 mile to the top, where there is a good view. The distance is 4.2 miles each way.

The section of the **Long Trail** from Middlebury Gap to Lincoln Gap, which includes the section described above, is 17.5 miles, and can be done in a day by strong hikers.

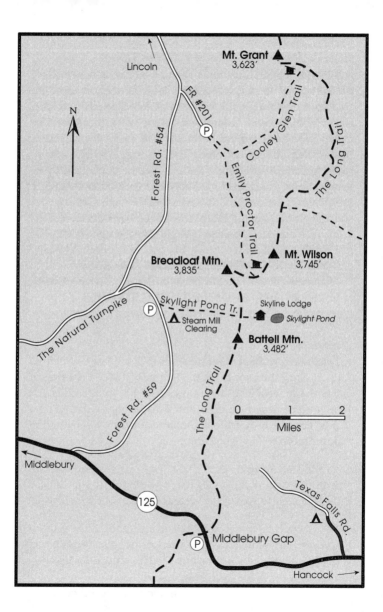

Skylight Pond and Battell Mtn. (3,482')

The Skylight Pond Trail provides quick access to **Skyline Lodge**, a nice cabin nestled above Skylight Pond. Both are just east of the Long Trail. From the parking area, walk up the gentle woods road for about 20 minutes, when it will begin to steepen. After a steady climb, there are views through the trees just before reaching the Long Trail (2.3 miles). Straight on is the trail to the cabin and the pond. To your right (LT south), the spur trail (right) to Battell Lookout, with good views west, is 250' away. Descend by the same route.

4 hours, 5 miles, elevation gain: 1,400' (Skyline Lodge)
Approach: From Ripton (east of Middlebury on Rt. 125), take Forest Rd.#59 (left) 3.6 miles to the trailhead.
Some may want to continue 1.1 miles north on the LT to **Breadloaf Mtn.**, where there is a good view. At 3,835', it is the highest point between Lincoln and Middlebury Gaps.

Rob. Frost Lookout and Worth Mtn. (3,234')

From Middlebury Gap, hike south on the Long Trail, passing through the Middlebury College Snow Bowl Ski Area. Ski trails are crossed seven times. Actually, the best views on the entire trip are from the first and last of these ski trail crossings! The first clearing has excellent views to the west, and the last one has good views to the east. After leaving the ski area, the trail steepens, soon reaching Robert Frost Lookout with a view to the west. After passing a few more minor lookouts, the viewless, wooded summit of Worth Mountain is reached. Return by the same route.

4.5 hours and 5.4 miles round trip. Elevation gain: 1,300'
Approach: From Middlebury, drive to East Middlebury, then up Route 125 to Middlebury Gap.

Lake Dunmore and Branbury State Park

Nestled at the foot of the Green Mountains, between Middlebury and Brandon, Lake Dunmore is a very popular swimming and boating spot. Of the several hikes in the area, Rattlesnake Point offers the best views. The less strenuous hike to beautiful Silver Lake is also a favorite.

Rattlesnake Point

This moderate hike leads to spectacular views of Lake Dunmore and Silver Lake. Not an actual summit, Rattlesnake Point is a group of ledges looming high above the lake. From the popular **Falls of Lana** (only about 15–20 minutes walk), follow signs to Rattlesnake Cliff—it is about 1.6 miles farther on. The excellent trail climbs briskly, then eases before climbing very steeply for a short distance to the spur trail, which leads left to the ledge overlooks. Both viewpoints should be visited, although the south lookout has a wider and more varied view. Unlike many precipitous dropoffs, these roomy ledges are inviting places to sit and relax.

3 hours and 4.5 miles round trip. Elevation gain: 1,100'
Approach: A short distance south of the park entrance are two parking areas on the left. Both are trailheads for the Falls of Lana, but the second (farther) one is the main one.
Variation: From Rattlesnake Point, the trail continues for 1.5 miles to **Mount Moosalamoo**, where there are some views, but the views are more dramatic from Rattlesnake Point.

Ski trail from Goshen to Ripton

A popular section of the **Catamount Ski Trail** passes just east of Lake Dunmore. From Route 73, west of Brandon Gap, it runs north through Blueberry Hill's trail network, crossing Route 125 at Middlebury College's Breadloaf Campus.

Cape Lookout Mountain 3,298'

This hike includes the spectacular views of Brandon Gap from popular **Mount Horrid Overlook**. From the parking area, cross the highway, and following the Long Trail north up through a fine birch forest, reach the spur trail (right) to the overlook after about 20 minutes. Walk out on the ledge for the view. *Note:* Because of Peregrine Falcon nesting, access to the top of the cliff might be closed from spring to late summer. Continue on the LT over **Mount Horrid** to the top of Cape Lookout Mountain. There are a couple of interesting viewpoints along the way. Return by the same route.

3 hours, 3.4 miles round trip. Elev. gain: 1,300'

Approach: From Brandon, drive east 8 miles on Route 73 to Brandon Gap. Parking is on the south side of Route 73.

From Rochester (on Rt. 100), Brandon Gap is 10 miles west.

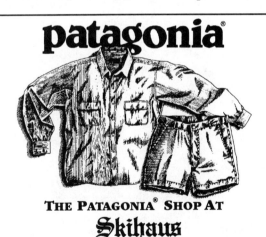

Killington and Nearby Hikes

Killington Peak, together with its various satellite peaks, is one of Vermont's largest mountains. It is also the home of the East's largest ski area, and the ski trails offer the hiker open slopes with great views. The Long Trail/Appalachian Trail passes through here, and just north of busy Route 4, the trails separate—the AT heading east to New Hampshire, and the LT continuing north to Canada.

Killington Peak 4,241'

The most popular hiking trail up Vermont's second highest mountain is the **Bucklin Trail** (blue blazes), which ascends from the west. The first 2 miles are along a gentle woods road and make for easy walking. After branching (right) off the road, the trail climbs very steeply all the way to **Cooper Lodge** on the Long Trail, slackening only a short ways below the lodge. From here, continue for 0.2 mile (steep) to the open, rocky summit with fine views in all directions, although various antennas clutter the view to the southeast. Descend by the same trail.

5–6 hours and 7.2 miles round trip. Elevation gain: 2,480'
Approach: 5 miles east on Route 4 (from Rt. 7 in Rutland), turn right on Wheelerville Road. Drive in 4 miles and park.
Ski trail variation: From the Killington Base Lodge, hike up under the Killington Peak double chairlift. As you ascend the very steep, grassy ski run, a fine view gradually unfolds. This "alpine" hiking terrain offers a pleasant change from our typical forest trails.
Time and approach: Drive to the upper end of the Killington Access Road. The hike up will take 1–2 hours. The chairlift is in operation throughout the summer.

Cooper Lodge on Killington Peak

Pico Peak 3,957'

Although lower than Killington, Pico's location and attractive symmetrical shape make it more noticeable, especially from the Rutland side. It offers good hiking with interesting views from the summit. Pico is also easily climbed by hiking the ski trails. For the Long Trail route, head south from Sherburne Pass. After about 20 minutes, there is a short side trail to the top of a chairlift and a view. At 2.5 miles you reach **Pico Camp**, a small cabin for Long Trail hikers. From here, the **Pico Link** side trail branches right and climbs steeply for 0.4 mile to the top of **Pico Peak**. Return by the Long Trail or descend one of the ski runs. To climb to the top of Killington Peak, continue south on the Long Trail for about 2 hours.

4 hours, 5.8 miles round trip. Elevation gain: 1,810'
Approach: Take Route 4 to Sherburne Pass (2,150'), where the Long Trail and Appalachian Trail cross the highway.

Deer Leap Rock

The interesting cliffs directly above Sherburne Pass on Route 4 provide a dramatic view of **Pico Peak** and the highway just below. To get to the top of the cliffs, follow the Long Trail and Appalachian Trail north for 0.5 mile to Maine Junction, where the two trails separate. Just beyond, left off the LT, the **Deer Leap Trail** climbs pleasantly through open woods, reaching a junction after 0.4 mile. Head left for 0.2 mile to the viewpoint, and then return the same way. At the upper junction, the other fork loops back down to the LT, at a point 1.3 miles from Route 4. Note: For safety reasons the steep, rough scramble up the cliffs has been closed by the Forest Service.

2 hours and 2.2 miles round trip. Elevation gain: 650'
Approach: Park next to the Long Trail Inn at Sherburne Pass on Route 4, about 10 miles east of Rutland.

Shrewsbury Peak 3,720'

This eastern satellite peak of Killington offers good hiking in a less-visited area. From the parking area, the blue-blazed **Shrewsbury Peak Trail** makes a short climb, then descends briefly before resuming its steady climb to the top. There are no viewpoints along the way, but from the summit there are excellent views to the south. Descend by the same trail. From the top of Shrewsbury, it is just a short way to the **Black Swamp Trail**, and about 2 miles on to the Long Trail. The Black Swamp Trail descends (right) for 1.5 miles to Black Swamp Road. It is then about 2.2 miles by road back to the base of the Shrewsbury Peak Trail.

3 hours, 3.6 miles round trip. Elevation gain: 1,500'
Approach: From Rt. 100, 3 miles south of Rt. 4, turn right on the CCC Road for 3.3 miles to parking on the right. From the west, the trailhead is 3 miles east of North Shrewsbury.

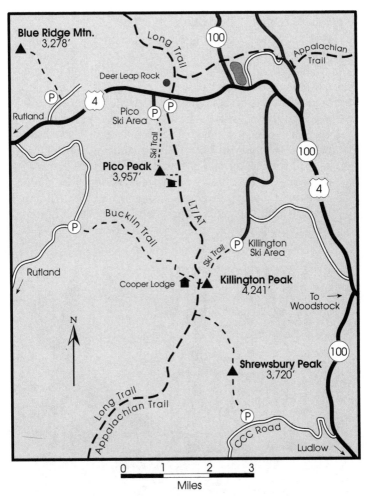

Maps: *USGS Killington Peak 1:24 000 and*
USGS Rutland 1:100 000 (metric).

Blue Ridge Mountain 3,278'

Located northwest of Killington and Pico, the rocky summit of Blue Ridge Mountain offers views of Rutland, Killington, and nearby mountains. From Turnpike Road, follow blue blazes along a woods road past a large camp building and onto the **Canty Trail**. The trail is gradual at first, then climbs steeply along a brook for a while before climbing over easier terrain through some nice woods to a clearing and the summit. By continuing a short way beyond the summit, you will be rewarded with better views. Descend by the same trail.

3.5 hours and 4.8 miles round trip. Elevation gain: 1,500'

Approach: About 6 miles east of Rutland, turn left off Route 4 on to Turnpike Road, and proceed for 0.7 mile to a gated road on the left. Park on the road shoulder.

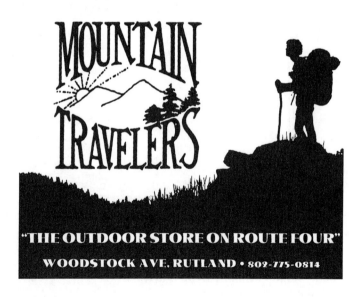

Mount Ascutney Area

The isolated shape of Mount Ascutney (3,150') is one of Vermont's best-known landmarks. Located in the town of Windsor, near the Connecticut River, Ascutney is unchallenged by other peaks, and is clearly visible for many miles throughout New Hampshire and Vermont. Although Ascutney is lower than many Vermont summits, its relative isolation and solid vertical rise contribute to make this one of the best mountain views in Vermont. In geologic terms, Mount Ascutney is a classic monadnock. Formerly the site of extensive granite quarrying and logging, Ascutney is today a recreation destination. In addition to Mount Ascutney Ski Area and Mount Ascutney State Park, there are four hiking trails to the top, a hang glider launch area, and a paved toll road to the 2,750' level.

Mount Ascutney via Brownsville Trail

An excellent and varied hike, the Brownsville Trail starts out steeply, then follows a moderately graded road to an old granite quarry. After negotiating some rougher terrain, the trail settles into a steady climb passing various viewpoints, and joins with the **Windsor Trail**, before reaching the summit observation tower. From a clearing 0.2 mile before the tower, a short spur leads right to **Brownsville Rock** with its bird's-eye view of the surrounding area. Descend by the same route, or by the Windsor Trail. (See Windsor Trail description.)

4.5 hours and 6.4 miles round trip. Elevation gain: 2,400'
Approach: From the village of Windsor, drive 4.6 miles west on Route 44, and park in the small trailhead parking lot on the south side of the highway.

Mount Ascutney from Killington

Ascutney via Weathersfield Trail

The blue-blazed Weathersfield Trail passes two cascades and numerous viewpoints on its varied route to the top. In particular, 84-foot-high **Crystal Cascade** (at 1.2 miles) is note-worthy, as it reveals Ascutney's geologic origins. **Gus' Lookout** (2,700'), at 2.3 miles, is open to the south, and at 2.6 miles, a short spur trail leads to **West Peak** with its excellent views. Take the left fork just before the summit to reach the observation tower and its 360-degree vista. Descend by the same route. Mount Ascutney's mid-state location provides a perfect spot to view the southern and northern Green Mountains, as well as the mountains of New Hampshire.

4 hours and 5.8 miles round trip. Elevation gain: 2,060'
Approach: Drive 3.3 miles west on Route 131 from the Ascutney exit on I-91, turn right on to Cascade Falls Rd., and follow signs to the trailhead parking.

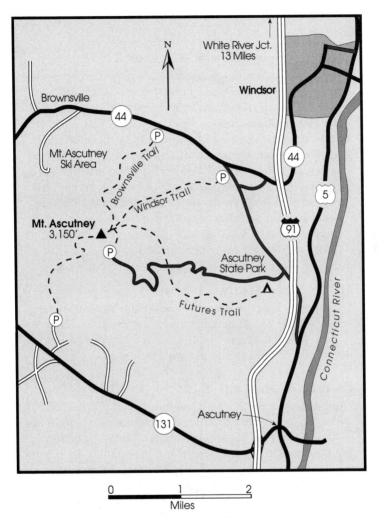

The ***Mount Ascutney Guide*** gives a history of the mountain and detailed trail information with two maps. The Ascutney Trails Association of Windsor, Vermont publishes it.

Mount Ascutney via Windsor Trail

Originally a road, this popular trail is the most direct route to the top. From Route 44A, the trail starts out in a field, but soon enters the woods and climbs more steeply. On this long-used route (white blazes), one passes the sites of old cabins and various dramatic episodes of yesteryear. At about 2.5 miles, the stone hut clearing is reached (take the short detour right to spectacular **Brownsville Rock**), and the summit tower is just beyond. Descend by the same trail or by Brownsville Trail. The road distance between the two trailheads is 1.2 miles.

4.5 hours and 5.4 miles round trip. Elevation gain: 2,520'
Approach: From Windsor, drive about 3.5 miles west on Route 44 to Route 44A. Then turn left on to Route 44A for a short distance to the trail parking lot on your right.

Hikes near Mount Ascutney

Two nearby hikes, **Okemo Mountain** and **Mount Tom**, are described below. In nearby Caanan, New Hampshire is popular **Mount Cardigan** (3,121'), a classic beginner hike to a beautiful, open, rocky summit with wide views.

Okemo Mountain 3,343' (Ludlow)

From the tower on Okemo's summit, the hiker is rewarded with a 360-degree view of mountains near and far. Completed in 1993 by Vermont's Youth Conservation Corps, the **Healdville Trail** ascends the north side of the mountain over mixed terrain. The first third climbs moderately, followed by an easier section before the final steeper climb to the top. Stay right at the junction near the top. Descend by the same trail.

4 hours and 5.8 miles round trip. Elevation gain: 1,940'
Approach: From Ludlow, drive north on Route 100 to Route 103. Continue 3 miles on Route 103 to Station Road, turn left and proceed 0.8 mile to the trailhead parking area.

Mount Tom 1,250' (Woodstock)

A pleasant, very gently graded path, complete with occasional benches, leads to the top of Woodstock's local mountain. It is the sort of path you would expect to find on a mountainside in Europe. Pick up the trail at the rear of **Faulkner Park**, and after many switchbacks you crest a knoll just below the summit. Continue a short ways on a steeper and rougher path to the actual top of Mt. Tom, where there are excellent views of Woodstock and the surrounding area. *2 hours and 3 miles round trip. Elevation gain: 550'*
Approach: Drive or walk to Faulkner Park, on Mountain Avenue, across the covered bridge in Woodstock.

Maps: *USGS 1:24 000 for Windsor, Woodstock* and
             USGS Claremont 1:100 000 (metric).

Manchester & Stratton Mountain

Manchester lies in the valley formed by the Taconic Range to the west, and the Green Mountain Range to the east. In this area, most of the mountain hiking is linked to the Long Trail, with the Taconics offering a few trails. An exception is impressive Mount Equinox, which looms directly over Manchester. Farther south, the Taconics have a more developed trail system, the Taconic Crest Trail.

Mt. Equinox 3,825'

Mt. Equinox rises almost 3,000' above Manchester, and is arguably the most impressive mountain in the area, Stratton included. The **Burr and Burton Trail**, the standard hiking route up the mountain, has received only sporadic maintenance in recent years, but the situation is improving. From the parking area, the blue-blazed trail first follows a woods road, but soon branches right and begins its steady climb. After about 2 miles, the trail is less steep, and at 2.7 miles, the intersection with the **Yellow Trail** and **Red Trail** is reached. The Yellow Trail offers a pleasant detour (right) for 0.5 mile over easy terrain to **Lookout Rock**, where there are excellent views. From here, take **Lookout Rock Trail** on to the summit and the Skyline Inn (upper end of the Equinox Toll Road). To descend, take Lookout Rock Trail for 0.1 mile, then turn right on the Burr and Burton Trail, and take it back down.

5–6 hours and 5.8 miles round trip. Elevation gain: 2,880'
Approach: From Manchester Center, drive south on Rt. 7A for a mile, and turn right on Seminary Street. Park behind the school. The trail starts from the upper parking lot.

Mount Equinox at sunrise

Prospect Rock 2,179'

Perhaps the favorite short hike in the area, Prospect Rock offers great views of Manchester, Mount Equinox, and to the north, Dorset Peak. From the gate at the end of the public road, start up the steep and rocky roadway (Old Rootville Road), and continue for about 1.5 miles to the Long Trail. The spur trail to Prospect Rock is about 200' farther south on the Long Trail. Return by the way you came.

2.5 hours and 3 miles round trip. Elevation gain: 1,000'
Approach: Drive east from Manchester Ctr. (on Rts. 11/30), turning right on East Manchester Road, then left on Rootville Road. There is very limited parking at the end of the road.

Lye Brook Falls is a popular, moderate hike (2.3 miles each way) to one of Vermont's highest waterfalls. Take the well-marked Lye Brook Trail off Glen Rd., in Manchester Ctr.

Stratton Mountain 3,936'

The conventional hiking route up Stratton is from the south, via the Long Trail, although climbing the mountain from the ski area (north side) is also recommended. The fire tower on the top of Stratton's South Peak, 0.8 mile south of the gondola terminal, provides a panoramic view extending to five states. From the parking area on Kelley Stand Road, follow the LT north for 3.3 miles to the tower. From the summit, the LT descends (left) 2.6 miles to beautiful **Stratton Pond**, a popular stopover with LT/AT thru-hikers. There are several shelters, and during hiking season, GMC caretakers are in residence. Return to the car via the gradually descending 4-mile **Stratton Pond Trail** (blue blazes), which ends on Kelley Stand Road, a mile west of your starting point.

7–8 hours and 11 miles round trip. Elevation gain: 1,910'
Approach: From Arlington, drive east, or from the *village of Stratton*, drive west on the Arlington–West Wardsboro Road (Kelley Stand Road) to the Long Trail parking area.

Spruce Peak 2,040'

Head south on the LT/AT over generally easy terrain, with only a 240' net gain in elevation from the highway. There are a couple of viewpoints along the way, and from the short spur trail (right) on Spruce Peak, there is a fine view to the west of Mount Equinox and the valley below. Return by the same route for a popular and quite easy hike. **Spruce Peak Shelter**, one of the finest cabins on the LT, lies 0.5 mile farther south, and is at a somewhat higher elevation than Spruce Peak.

2–2.5 hours and 4.5 miles round trip. Elevation gain: 240'
Approach: From Manchester Center, drive 5 miles on Routes 11/30 to the Long Trail highway crossing and park.

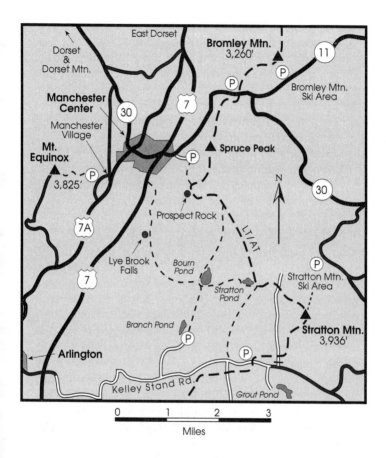

Maps: *USGS 1:24 000 Dorset* and *Stratton Mountain,*
USGS Glens Falls 1:100 000 (metric),
USFS Green Mountain Forest, Southern Half, and
Recreation Map & Guide for Bennington County.

Bromley Mountain 3,260'

Hike north on the Long Trail/Appalachian Trail over generally moderate terrain to reach the top of Bromley, where there is a cafeteria and plenty of deck space. The views south to Stratton Ski Area and of the other nearby mountains are excellent. Descend by the same route, or, as an alternative to trail walking, hike down the steep, grassy ski trails to the base of the ski area. (Arrange a car shuttle.)

4 hours and 5.6 miles round trip. Elevation gain: 1,460'

Approach: From Manchester Center, drive east on Routes 11 and 30 for 5 miles to the large parking area on the left, which is where the Long Trail crosses the highway.

Griffith Lake and Baker Peak 2,850'

Although well below treeline, Baker has a rocky, exposed summit with a sweeping westerly view, from Equinox in the south to Dorset Peak (directly across the valley) and many miles to the north. From your car, hike up the **Lake Trail** (moderately steep) reaching **Baker Peak Trail** at 2 miles, after crossing McGinn Brook. After a mile of mostly easy walking (a few steep parts), you reach the Long Trail. Head left (north) on the Long Trail for 0.1 mile to the top. Descend either by the same route, or head south on the Long Trail (easy terrain) for 1.9 miles to lovely **Griffith Lake**. From the lake, backtrack on the LT to the Lake Trail, and follow it down to the car.

Loop: 5–6 hours, 9 miles round trip. Elevation gain: 2,350'

Approach: From Manchester, drive north on Route 7, 2.4 miles past Emerald Lake to Town Highway 5. Turn right, and park on the left after 0.5 mile.

Map Reference: See page 101 for the map showing this hike.

Dorset Peak 3,770'

The trail up this attractive, steep-sided (but viewless) peak is not maintained; however, it is climbed regularly. Dorset Peak is one of New England's 100 highest peaks, and is a requirement for those on that particular quest. Similar in appearance to Equinox, it is very prominent from Route 7 when approaching from the north. The first mile of the route is negotiable with a 4-wheel drive vehicle. From a logging clearing, the trail ascends steeply past a hunting camp, and continues to the saddle west of the summit before contouring around to the north. This trip is recommended only for hikers who are very experienced with route finding.

5 hours and 7 miles round trip. Elevation gain: 2,300'

Approach: From Dorset (west of Manchester Center), follow Dorset Hollow Road, then Tower Road to the end of the valley, about 4 miles from Dorset. The trailhead is unmarked.

Bennington Area

Bennington is in the southwestern corner of the state, only 11 miles from Massachusetts. The main ridge of the Green Mountains lies a few miles to the east, while the Taconic Range is immediately to the west along the New York border. We describe several Bennington favorites as well as two hikes approached from Massachusetts. One of them, Mount Greylock (3,491'), is *in* Massachusetts. Since it is only 14 miles south of Bennington and a very important hiking area, we describe one of Greylock's most popular routes.

Harmon Hill 2,320'

Harmon Hill is a popular Bennington hike, giving good, close views of the town and the nearby Taconic mountains. The Forest Service keeps the summit area clear of brush by annual controlled burns. From the parking on Route 9, head south on the Long Trail, at times quite steeply, reaching the top of Harmon Hill at about 1.7 miles. The steep sections of the trail use rock and log steps. Return by the same route.

2.5 hours and 3.4 miles round trip. Elevation gain: 1,265'
Approach: From Bennington, drive east on Route 9 for 5 miles to the Long Trail crossing and the trailhead parking.

Maps: *USGS 1:24 000 Manchester, Dorset, Stratton Mtn.,*
USFS Green Mtn. Nat. Forest, Southern Half,
Mount Greylock State Reservation Trail Map, and
Recreation Map & Guide to Bennington County.

Bald Mountain 2,857'

The 7-mile **Bald Mtn. Trail** starts on North Branch Street in Bennington and traverses Bald Mountain, ending in Woodford Hollow, on the east side of the mountain. The shorter option is from the Woodford side. From your car, follow the blue-blazed trail first along old road beds, then up through a series of switchbacks, reaching the **West Ridge Trail** at 2.5 miles. Head right (north) for 0.1 mile to reach the top. There are good views of Bennington and the nearby mountains from various viewpoints near the summit. Return by the same route. The West Ridge Trail continues north, then east, for 7.6 miles to meet the Long Trail near Goddard Shelter on Glastenbury Mountain. See the loop hike described below.

4 hours and 5.2 miles roundtrip. Elevation gain: 1,600'
Approach: From Bennington, drive east 4 miles on Route 9 to the Woodford church. Head left on a gravel road for 0.8 mile to the trailhead, at a concrete water tank (on the left).

Glastenbury Mountain 3,747'

From Route 9, hike north on the LT/AT, most of the time in dense woods, passing two outlooks along the way. Plan to overnight at **Goddard Shelter** (lean-to with room for 10 people), 9.8 miles from the car. The summit and observation tower are 0.3 mile beyond the shelter. The view is one of a huge forest expanse, with few signs of man's intrusion upon nature. Return the next day by the same route, or, more interestingly, by the **West Ridge Trail** over **Bald Mountain** and down to Woodford (see above). The Bald Mountain variation takes a little longer.

12–13 hours (2 days), 20-mile loop, elevation gain: 2,400'
Approach: From Bennington, drive 5 miles east on Route 9 to the parking area where the Long Trail crosses the highway.

The Dome 2,748'

From the trailhead, follow the **Dome Trail** for 2.9 miles to the summit of Dome. At 1.5 miles, the **Agawon Trail** comes in from the right. The final half mile of the trail is rocky and interesting, and from the exposed rocks on the summit, there are good views of Mount Greylock and southern Vermont. The Dome Trail, blazed in orange, is maintained by the Williams Outing Club. The WOC maintains the trails in the Williamstown area and produces a guide book describing over 30 trails, including the Dome and Mount Greylock.

3.5 hours and 5.8 miles round trip. Elevation gain: 1,700'
Approach: From Route 7, 1.5 miles south of the Vt.-Mass. border, turn left (east) on Sand Springs Rd. At White Oaks Rd., turn left; park after 1.5 miles, 0.3 mile back inside Vermont.

Mount Greylock 3,491' (Massachusetts)

The highest mountain in the state, Greylock is an impressive sight. It is graced with many hiking trails, including the Appalachian Trail. Popular **Bascom Lodge**, on the top, is an important milestone for AT thru-hikers. The **Hopper Trail**, perhaps the classic route, climbs steeply up the north flank of the Hopper, a huge ravine on the west side. From the parking area, walk first along easy terrain before bearing right and climbing, reaching Sperry Rd. after about an hour (2 miles). The route then merges with Deer Hill Trail, passing Rockwell Rd. twice before meeting the AT (white blazes). Follow this to the summit. Return by the same route.

5 hours and 8.2 miles round trip. Elevation gain: 2,340'
Approach: From Williamstown (south of Bennington), drive east on Rt. 2 for a short distance before turning right onto Water St. Continue south for 2.6 miles, then turn left on Hopper Road; follow this 2.7 miles to the parking area.

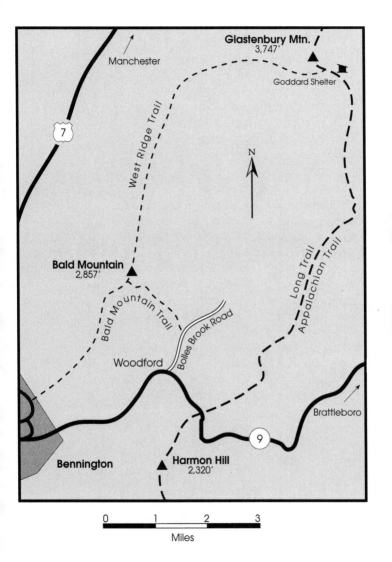

Glastenbury Mtn.
3,747'

Goddard Shelter

Manchester

West Ridge Trail

7

N

Bald Mountain
2,857'

Bald Mountain Trail

Bolles Brook Road

Long Trail
Appalachian Trail

Woodford

Brattleboro

9

Bennington

Harmon Hill
2,320'

0   1   2   3
Miles

Mount Snow Area

We give four hikes in the southeastern corner of the state and two in New Hampshire. Mount Olga, Mount Snow, and Haystack Mountain are all near Wilmington. Bald Mountain enjoys relative isolation in Townshend State Park, northwest of Brattleboro, off Route 30. Mt. Wantastiquet, just across the river from Brattleboro, along with fabled Mount Monadnock, east of Keene, complete the chapter.

Mount Snow 3,556'

Mt. Snow is the home of a large alpine ski area, which in the summer is a major mountain biking center. Generally not as steep as many other alpine areas, Mount Snow is excellent terrain for mountain biking. Climb the mountain by the ski trails, which offer hiking on open, grassy slopes. From the rocky summit, there are extensive views of southern Vermont and Massachusetts, and New Hampshire's Mount Monadnock is easily picked out. There is an excellent view of nearby Somerset Reservoir. The gondola runs during the summer, giving one the option of riding up and walking down.

2.5 hours and 3 miles roundtrip. Elevation gain: 1,500'
Approach: From Wilmington, drive north on Route 100 to Mount Snow. Park at the ski area base lodge.

The **Deerfield Trail** connects the top of Mt. Snow with the top of Haystack Ski Area. Primarily a cross country ski and snowmobile trail, this 3-mile trail segment is negotiable in summer, but is quite rough and therefore something for more experienced and self-sufficient hikers.

Maps: *USGS 1:24 000 Mt. Snow, Townshend* and
 USGS 1:100 000 Keene (metric).

Haystack Pond

Haystack Mountain 3,420'

Haystack Mountain is one of the more popular and interesting mountain hikes in southeastern Vermont. It is a satellite of Mount Snow, but for hikers Haystack has more significance. From the summit, there is a good view of **Haystack Pond** about 500' below, as shown above. Many of the mountains of southern Vermont can be seen, and Mount Greylock in western Massachusetts, is also visible. Once the trailhead is located, the blue-blazed trail is easy to follow. Carefully note trail intersections on the way up for your return trip.

3 hours and 4.8 miles. Elevation gain: 1,030'

Approach: From Wilmington, drive west on Rt. 9 for 1.1 miles, and turn right on Haystack Rd. Continue on Haystack, staying right, to Chimney Hill Rd. at about 1.2 miles. Turn left here, then right on Binney Brook Rd. Stay on this, and at 2.6 miles from Rt. 9, reach the trailhead on the right.

Mount Olga 2,415'

From the fire tower on Mount Olga's wooded summit there are sweeping views. The loop trail from **Molly Stark State Park** is blue-blazed and easy to follow. Mount Olga can also be climbed directly from Route 9, up the open ski trails (good views) of Hogback Ski Area. For those with less time, this alternative is shorter and offers less climbing.

Loop: 1.5 hours and 1.6 miles. Elevation gain: 500'
Approach: Mount Olga is located in Molly Stark State Park, 3.4 miles east of Wilmington, just south of Route 9. It is about 14 miles west of Brattleboro.

Bald Mountain 1,680'

This modest mountain offers a good hike with a moderate climb. There are views of Bromley, Stratton, and the West River Valley from the summit. The trail starts from the campground, crossing and recrossing a brook before reaching the top after about 1.4 miles. The standard loop is done by descending the mountain via the steeper north side trail, which returns to the campground.

Loop: 2.5 hours and 2.8 miles. Elevation gain: 1,100'
Approach: From Townshend (20 miles from Brattleboro), drive west on Rt. 30. Cross the river at Townshend Dam, and turn left back along the river (passing Vermont's longest single span covered bridge) to Townshend State Park.
Map: A free hiker's map is available at the campground.

Mt. Wantastiquet 1,351' (near Brattleboro)

Although not in Vermont, Mount Wantastiquet is Brattleboro's local hike. In fact, it is easy to walk from town to the top. From the parking area, follow the road to the top where there are good views of the area.

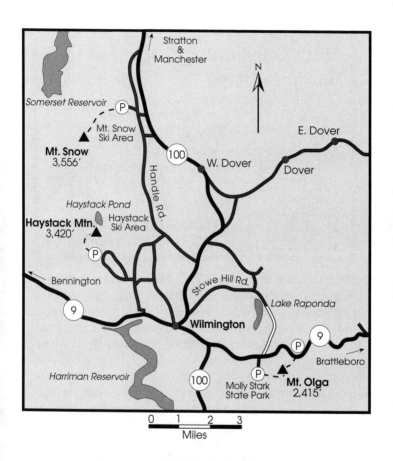

1.5 hours and 1.4 miles round trip. Elevation gain: 1,200'
Approach: From Brattleboro, cross the Connecticut River into New Hampshire, and take the left *immediately* after the bridge. Park at the gate after about a quarter of a mile.

Mt. Monadnock 3,165' (New Hampshire)

Ascending from the west, the **Marlboro Trail** starts out with easy grades, but steepens, alternating between forest pockets and open rock ledges. About a half-mile from the top, the summit area comes into view, and the **Dublin Trail** enters from the left. The upper part of Monadnock is a fantastic expanse of bare rock—the result of fires over a hundred years ago—and in good weather is a great place to hang out. Descend by the same route, carefully noting trail intersections. The Marlboro Trail receives much less traffic than the trails from Monadnock State Park.

3 1/4 hours and 4.4 miles. Elevation gain: 1,865'

Approach: Although 35 miles from Brattleboro, and well inside New Hampshire, Monadnock draws many hikers from southern Vermont. From NH 124, 5 miles east of Marlboro, head left 0.7 miles on Shaker Farm Rd. to trailhead.

Groton State Forest

This popular recreation area is located east of Montpelier. It is heavily forested, but the numerous lakes and some interesting granitic outcrops make it an area worth exploring. The state park (within the state forest) has several campgrounds and a network of hiking trails, as well as other recreation possibilities. There is a day usage fee, but a free trail guide and map is available at the park entrance.

Approach: From Barre, take Route 302 east to Route 232, turn left and drive past Lake Groton to Groton State Park.

Owl's Head 1,958'

This is a popular hike with great views of Lake Groton and beautiful Kettle Pond. On the top, trails on smooth granite bedrock radiate in all directions through spruces and blueberry bushes. The hiking trail begins off the road to **Osmore Pond**, and after avoiding a swampy area, climbs up to a parking area. It is then a steep 0.1 mile to the top.

1.5 hours and 3 miles round trip. Elevation gain: 230'

Approach: From New Discovery Campground B, follow signs to the trail. *Note:* The easy way to "hike" Owl's Head is to drive up the gravel road, which goes to within 0.1 mile of the actual summit.

Big Deer Mountain 1,992'

Big Deer is similar to Owl's Head, but offers a slightly higher and less-visited summit with excellent views of nearby lakes and surrounding mountains. The first mile of the **Big Deer Mountain Trail** is quite easy, with the last half mile climbing steeply up to the summit area. The trail has blue blazes.

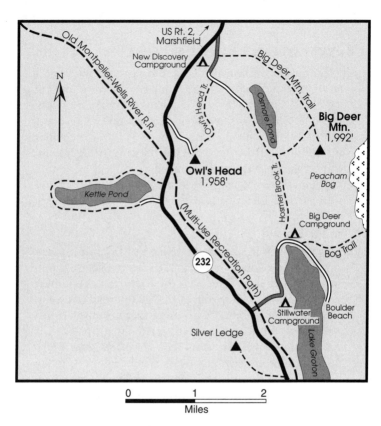

2 hours and 3.4 miles round trip. Elevation gain: 250'
Approach: Drive through the park entrance to where
Campground B begins, and turn left on the road to **Peacham
Pond** for 0.3 mile. The trailhead is on the right with limited
parking.

Maps: *USGS 1:24 000 Marshfield, Knox Mountain and
USGS 1:100 000 (metric) Montpelier.*

Spruce Mountain 3,037'

Located at the western edge of Groton State Forest, only the summit of Spruce is in the Forest, and the mountain is some distance away from Lake Groton. From the gate, follow the woods road to the right, staying on it for about a mile as it swings around to the south side of the mountain. At 1.5 miles, the trail begins a more or less steady climb to the top, at times passing across exposed granite. From the tower on the summit, there are excellent views in all directions. Descend by the same route. Nearby **Signal Mountain**, at 3,348', is the highest mountain in this range, but there is no hiking trail to the summit.

3 hours 4.4 miles round trip. Elevation gain: 1,340'
Approach: From Plainfield, drive south on East Hill Road for 4.3 miles and turn left on Spruce Mtn. Rd. Turn left at the next junction, and continue uphill to the gate and parking.

Kettle Pond Trail

This pleasant hike skirts the shoreline of a beautiful, secluded pond. It takes an hour or two and is a good hike for families. The trail is somewhat rocky and wet at the far end of the pond. Starting from the highway, walk around the pond in a clockwise fashion, ending at the Kettle Pond Group Camping Area just south of where you began the hike.

1–2 hours, 3-mile loop. Elevation gain: negligible.
Approach: Parking on the west side of the road, about a mile south of the side road up Owl's Head.

The abandoned railroad bed of the old Montpelier-Wells River Railroad makes for excellent biking and hiking, and for skiing and snowmobiling in winter. See the map.

The Northern Frontier

The mountains traversed by the Long Trail from Route 15 north to Canada are referred to as the Northern Frontier. Although less visited than much of the terrain to the south, there is fine hiking in this wilder, more remote part of the state. A good deal of the trail runs across private land, and the Green Mountain Club is working with landowners to secure permanent protection for the Long Trail corridor.

Prospect Rock 1,040'

This is the short, popular hike near Johnson. Follow the Long Trail north, and climb steeply to the top of the south-facing ledges, where there are good local views of the Lamoille Valley and nearby hills. Return by the same route.

1–1.5 hours, 1.5 miles, elevation gain: 530'
Approach: From Johnson, drive west on Route 15: Turn right on to Hogback Road and park at Ithiel Camp. Take the Long Trail north—it starts out as a driveway.

Laraway Mountain 2,790'

Laraway Mountain is the highest summit along the crest of the Green Mountains between Route 15 (near Johnson) and Route 118. From the parking area at the end of Codding Hollow Road, take the Long Trail north. There is a good viewpoint at 2 miles with a very interesting view of Mount Mansfield, 15 miles to the south. The summit is reached at 2.4 miles. Descend by the same route.

3.5 hours and 4.8 miles round trip. Elevation gain: 1,550'
Approach: From Jeffersonville, drive north on Rt. 118 to Codding Hollow Rd., about 1.5 miles past Waterville. Follow it to the end (2.7 miles), staying left at 1.4 miles.

The Long Trail at treeline

Belvidere Mountain 3,360'

A fine, distinct mountain in an isolated setting, Belvidere offers a very worthwhile hike. On a windy day, the sensation from the 70' fire tower is like flying! The route follows the Long Trail north from Rt. 118, and offers pleasant walking on an interesting and varied trail. Although these more northerly trees are noticeably shorter, the views are limited until the top is reached. At Belvidere Saddle (3,200'), take the **Forester's Trail** 0.2 mile to the top. Return the way you came. The Forester's Trail descends from the saddle east to the asbestos mine access road, 4.5 miles north of Route 118.

   4 hours and 5.6 miles round trip. Elevation gain: 2,140'
   Approach: From Jeffersonville, drive north on Route 109, turn right on Route 118, and park where the Long Trail crosses the highway, near the height of land.

Maps: *USGS Hazen's Notch and Jay Peak (1:24 000)*
Note: *See page 97 for the map of this area.*

Burnt Mountain 2,725'

Burnt Mountain is off the "beaten path". Starting out as a woods road, the route passes several beaver ponds before narrowing to a blue-blazed trail. After a steeper section, you reach Window Rock with a good view of Hazen's Notch. Continue climbing steeply over rock ledges and through a beautiful paper birch stand to reach the wooded summit. By hiking 10–15 minutes beyond the actual summit to a cairn, you'll obtain an impressive 340-degree view. From this vantage point, the view of nearby Hazen's Notch (only 2 miles away) is perhaps the finest in the entire area. Return by the same trail.

3.5 hours and 4 miles round trip.

Approach: From Montgomery Center, drive 1.7 miles up Hazen's Notch Road. Turn right on Rossier Road and park at the end of the road.

Buchanan Mountain 2,940'

The 7-mile traverse of Buchanan Mountain offers several good viewpoints of Jay Peak and the surrounding mountains. From Hazen's Notch, head north on the Long Trail, passing Hazen's Notch Camp after a half mile, before beginning a steep climb. The summit of Buchanan is reached at 4 miles, with a good view of Jay Peak. **Chet's Lookout** (at 4.2 miles) and **Domey's Dome** (at 5.2 miles) both offer good views. After 7 miles, the Long Trail crosses Route 242 to begin its ascent of Jay Peak. Montgomery Center is about 6.5 miles away.

4 hours and 7 miles, one way from Hazen's Notch to Rt. 242.

Approach: From Montgomery Center, drive 5.5 miles up Hazen's Notch Road to Hazen's Notch.

Jay Peak 3,861'

With a large tram station adjacent to the summit, Jay does not provide an unspoiled wilderness experience. However, this hike traverses a fine section of the Long Trail, and the views from the summit are superb. Take the Long Trail north from the parking area on Rt. 242. The rocky, well-maintained trail climbs briskly through birches and into the spruce-fir zone. Near the top, the trail crosses a ski trail before the final climb to the bare rock summit. Descend by the same route. It is also possible to climb Jay by one of the ski trails. The tram is in operation during the summer.

3 hours and 3.4 miles round trip. Elevation gain: 1,680'

Approach: From Montgomery Center, drive 6.8 miles north on Route 242 (or 5 miles south from the village of Jay), and park at the trail head parking, just south of height of land.

Northeast Kingdom

The cool, deep waters of Lake Willoughby (a land-locked fjord) are a mecca for fishermen, while the cliffs of Mount Pisgah offer some of the best ice climbing in the Northeast. Although the summits are wooded and well below the treeline, the hikes in this region offer some of the most spectacular views in Vermont. Lake Willoughby is about 22 miles north of St. Johnsbury. Nearby Burke Mountain and the remote Mount Monadnock are also interesting.

Mount Pisgah 2,751'

Mount Pisgah is one of Vermont's more dramatic mountains, and the view of Lake Willoughby from the top of the 1,000' cliffs will not disappoint you. The popular **South Trail** leaves the highway and crosses a pond area on bridges. The trail then ascends very steeply, before passing perch-like **Pulpit Rock**, with its aerial view of the south end of the lake. The main trail is safe enough, but the wooded mountainside is extremely steep—use caution! After another sustained climb, the gradient eases before reaching a rock slab with sweeping views to the south. The wooded summit is just beyond, at 1.7 miles, where a spur trail leads right to an interesting view of Bald Mtn. From the top, descend a short way to reach the famous viewpoints (left) atop Pisgah's cliffs. They are larger and safer than Pulpit Rock. Descend the way you came up. The fine 2.2-mile **North Trail** also starts from Route 5A, at a point 3 miles north of South Trail's trailhead.

2.5 hours, 3.5 miles. Elevation gain: 1,450' (South Trail)
Approach: From Lyndonville, take Rt. 114 to West Burke, then Rt. 5A for 6 miles to a parking area (left) just south of Lake Willoughby. The South Trail begins across the highway.

Mount Pisgah from the south

Mount Hor 2,648'

Mount Hor is directly across Lake Willoughby from Mount Pisgah, and its main attraction is the spectacular view of the lake and Pisgah's cliffs. The blue-blazed trail does not actually go to the top of Mt. Hor, but does lead to several viewpoints. After 0.7 mile, the trail forks. Take the right fork another 0.7 mile to **East Lookout**, where there is a superb view of Mount Pisgah, and to **North Lookout**, with impressive views of the lake and north into Canada. The left fork climbs in 0.3 mile to **Summit Lookout**, with good views to the west.

2 hours and 2.8 miles round trip. Elevation gain: 700'

Approach: Turn left (west) off Route 5A, about 6 miles north of West Burke, and drive up a gravel road (the CCC Road) for 1.8 miles to a parking area on the right.

Wheeler Mountain 2,371'

This popular, short hike has the feel of a rock climb as you clamber up and across smooth granite slabs. After a short distance, the trail divides into the **Red Trail** (shorter, steeper) and the **White Trail**. They merge just below the top. Most hikers will enjoy the steeper ascent, followed by the slightly longer White Trail on the descent. After reaching the summit ledges, continue a few minutes to spectacular **Eagle Cliff** where there are better views towards Lake Willoughby and of the surrounding area. The clean granite slabs make this hike unusual for Vermont. A somewhat similar but longer hike is Maple Ridge on Mt. Mansfield.

2 hours and 2 miles round trip. Elevation gain: 700'
Approach: From Route 5, 8.3 miles north of West Burke, turn right on to Wheeler Pond Road, and drive for 2 miles to a small signed parking area on the left.

Bald Mountain 3,315'

With its summit tower, and as the highest mountain in the Lake Willoughby area, Bald Mtn. offers the best general views in the region. There are two routes to the summit (note map). The Long Pond route starts about 100 yards east of the pond access. Using various old woods roads, the trail ascends generally moderately to the summit with only limited views along the way. Descend by same trail.

3 hours and 4 miles round trip. Elevation gain: 1,450'
Approach: From Westmore (Lake Willoughby), drive 2 miles east on Long Pond Road to Long Pond and park at the lake access parking or just beyond, at the trailhead.
Haystack Mtn. (2,712') is easily climbed from Long Pond Road, and there are good views from the top. Park 0.6 mile past Long Pond access. *1–1.5 hours, 2 miles round trip.*

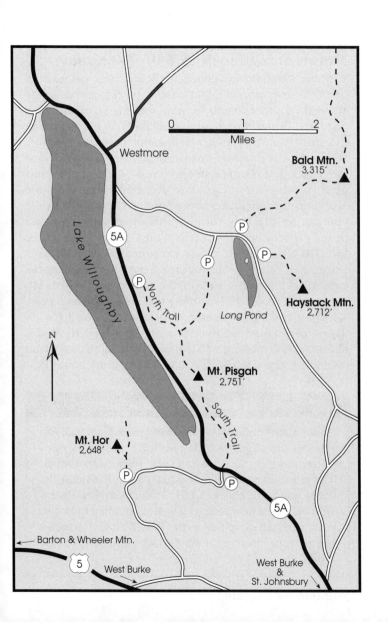

Westmore

0 1 2
Miles

Bald Mtn.
3,315'

Lake Willoughby

5A

P

North Trail

P

P

Long Pond

P

Haystack Mtn.
2,712'

N

Mt. Pisgah
2,751'

South Trail

Mt. Hor
2,648'

P

P

P

5A

← Barton & Wheeler Mtn.

5

West Burke

West Burke
&
St. Johnsbury ↓

Mount Monadnock 3,140' (Vermont)

Vermont's Mount Monadnock, in the extreme northeastern corner of the state, is a local landmark, rising over 2,000' above the Connecticut River. Although it is a fine hike, on a good trail, Monadnock is almost unknown to hikers outside the area. From the bridge, walk south along the highway about 100', and turn right on to a private road. This soon turns into a trail, and climbing steeply, crosses a stream (45 minutes), continues to climb steeply before slackening and reaching the summit after about 2 hours. The trail is viewless until the top. Climb the tower (needs repair) to get above the trees for spectacular views of the North Country, into Canada, and of New Hampshire's Mt. Washington and the Presidential Range. Analogous to Mt. Ascutney, both are monadnocks located on the west bank of the Connecticut River. Mt. Monadnock is only 10 feet lower than its southern cousin.

3.5 hours and 5 miles round trip. Elevation gain: 2,100'
Approach: Across the river from Colebrook, NH, Mount Monadnock is on Route 102, about 30 miles east of Island Pond. Park just south of the Route 26 bridge on Route 102.

What is a Monadnock ?

A monadnock is a mass of relatively hard bedrock (an igneous intrusion), which, surviving erosional forces better than the surrounding rock, forms a mountain. The word "monadnock" is actually an Indian name for the Mount Monadnock (3,165') in southern New Hampshire. Located near Keene, it is often claimed to be the most climbed mountain in the United States. Usage of the term has been extended to all mountains of this type.

Burke Mountain 3,267'

Home of Burke Mountain Ski Area, Burke also offers good hiking and mountain biking. There is a road to the top (hiking is allowed, car toll), but the best hiking route begins as a small road to the right of the ski area parking lot. After 0.8 mile, take the red-blazed trail (left), and climb about 800' to the fire road. Here, at a lean-to, the trail divides, with the blue-blazed route taking a steeper line to the summit ridge. The two trails rejoin about 50 feet below the top of West Peak. Follow the **Profile Trail** to the summit tower, where there are excellent views of Mount Pisgah and nearby mountains. Descend by same route, or by ski trails.

2.5 hours and 3.5 miles round trip. Elevation gain: 1,270'
Approach: From East Burke (just north of Lyndonville), continue 1 mile on Mountain Road to the Burke Mountain Sherburne Lodge parking lots.

Backcountry skiing

With the rediscovery of the telemark turn and today's excellent equipment, skiers are able to handle most terrain competently. Hiking trails (on Camel's Hump, for example) are often used for an ascent, before skiing down through open glades. And using waxed or "waxless" skis, we can cover miles and miles (skiers measure distances in kilometers) in good nordic fashion. While some backcountry areas are suitable for beginners (Little River, Nebraska Notch), skiers just starting out will do well to develop confidence at a touring center on groomed trails.

Mount Mansfield Region

With a trail network of over 200 miles, several challenging mountain traverses, steep and narrow alpine-style descents, miles of mellow woods skiing, and six interconnected cross country ski touring centers, the Stowe-Bolton-Underhill-Jeffersonville area is unequalled in New England. The classic trips are described below, and the map shows in a general way how the trails and ski centers relate to each other.

Bolton to Trapps Trail

This challenging tour from Bolton Valley Ski Area to Stowe is probably the classic backcountry ski tour in Vermont. It is done in either direction, but has less climbing and better telemarking when starting from Bolton. After leaving the ski area, you pass through a glade of birches, contour across the face of Bolton Mountain, and finally descend 2,000' into Nebraska Valley. There are dramatic views of Cottonbrook Basin and south to Camel's Hump. Continue to Trapps via the Old County Road to Russell Knoll and on to the ski shop. 20 km, 4-7 hours. A demanding tour in remote terrain.

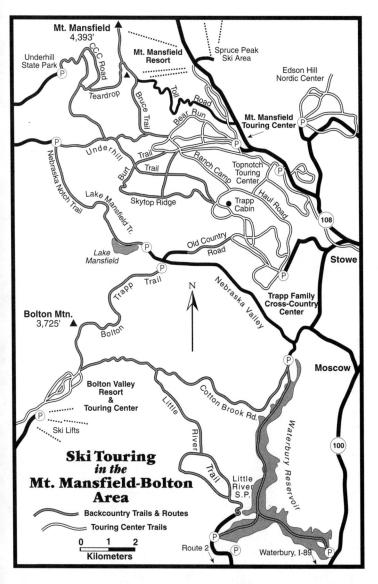

Mt. Mansfield
4,393'

Underhill
State Park
P

CCC Road

Mt. Mansfield
Resort

Spruce Peak
Ski Area

Edson Hill
Nordic Center

Teardrop

Bruce Trail

Bear Run

Toll Road

Mt. Mansfield
Touring Center

P

Underhill Trail

Burt Trail

Ranch Camp

Topnotch
Touring
Center

P

Nebraska Notch Trail

Lake Mansfield Tr.

Skytop Ridge

Trapp Cabin

Haul Road

108

Lake
Mansfield

P

Old Country Road

Stowe

P

Trapp Trail

N

Nebraska Valley

Trapp Family
Cross-Country
Center

Bolton Mtn.
3,725'

Bolton

P

Moscow

Bolton Valley
Resort
&
Touring Center

P

Ski Lifts

Little River Trail

Cotton Brook Rd.

Waterbury Reservoir

100

Ski Touring
in the
Mt. Mansfield-Bolton
Area

～～ Backcountry Trails & Routes

═══ Touring Center Trails

Little River
S.P.

0   1   2
Kilometers

P

Route 2

P

Waterbury, I-89

P

Skytop and Burt Trail Loop

A favorite, this trail ascends and traverses Skytop Ridge and ends at Dewey Saddle. It offers good viewpoints from short spur trails. Traveling a unique, high place in beautiful hardwoods, the trail starts from the **Haul Road**, just below **Trapps Cabin**. Initial steepness gives way into an undulating climb. Towards the end, it works its way through dense balsam firs before dropping steeply into Dewey Saddle. To finish the standard loop, head down Burt Trail, and then take a right on the **Underhill Trai**l, which returns to your starting point.

Burt Trail

A telemarker's dream in powder, the upper section provides exciting open woods skiing in some huge white birches. The trail drops 1,800' from Dewey Saddle into Ranch Valley. The **Steeple Trail** (extremely steep, drops off Skytop) and the **Dewey Trail** are somewhat similar to the Burt Trail. Skiing up the Overland Trail (then head left on the Underhill Trail) to access the Burt is a fine trip. These trails are most directly approached from the Mount Mansfield Touring Center.

Underhill Trail

Linking Underhill with the Trapp and Mt. Mansfield touring centers, this important trail lets you ski from the Burlington side of the mountain to Stowe. Generally of moderate difficulty (it is a traverse, basically), it does cross some very steep terrain between the Long Trail and the Burt Trail. Prevailing snow conditions can make a vast difference in difficulty. About 3–4 hours from Stevensville parking to Trapps.

Map reference: *Ski Touring Map and Guide to Stowe and the Mount Mansfield Region*

CCC Road

This route gives you a chance to see the imposing west side of Mount Mansfield. From the gate at Underhill State Park (or lower down, depending on current snow conditions), ski up the graded road for 2 miles to its end. Excellent for intermediates. 7 km. 2-3 hours. Moderately easy, although it can be rutted and icy. The hiking trails on Mansfield are generally much too steep and narrow to offer any skiing enjoyment.

W.B. Trail

From Underhill State Park, the trail traverses south, crossing the bottom of the Teardrop Trail, rounding Maple Ridge, and continuing to meet the Underhill Trail a short distance below the main ridge. Essentially it links the Underhill State Park area with Stowe. Difficulty: moderate. The trail is named for Warren Beeken and Wilbur Bull, to whom we also owe the Underhill Trail.

Nebraska Notch Trail

From the parking area at the end of Stevensville road (snow conditions may dictate parking lower down), take the Nebraska Notch hiking trail up a gentle climb and across easy terrain to the beaver ponds at the base of impressive Nebraska Notch. A popular 4-mile round trip for beginner and intermediate skiers.

Teardrop Trail (west side of Mt. Mansfield)

The area's classic ski descent plunges off Mansfield's summit ridge. Very steep and narrow at the top, it gradually relaxes its attack. It can be approached from the Octagon (Mt. Mansfield Ski Area), but most people ski up the **CCC Road** or the Lower Teardrop from Underhill State Park to the base of the Teardrop and ski up with climbing skins. Easily picked out from Underhill Center, it appears as a thin white line just north of Maple Ridge. Difficulty rating: Expert.

Bruce Trail

A less serious undertaking than Teardrop, the Bruce Trail is still a challenging run requiring quick reflexes. Beginning from the Octagon (take the lift), it drops 2,000' into Ranch Valley (Mt. Mansfield Touring Center), merging with the Overland Trail after a mile.

Little River State Park and Waterbury Reservoir

A bit farther afield—approached from Waterbury—the Little River area contains a fine network of trails and old roads in generally moderate terrain, i.e. good nordic skiing. The large reservoir (popular with ice fishermen) offers a total change from steep, wooded trails. The main route from the dam through to Moscow (groomed for snowmobiles) is excellent and can be combined with skiing the length of the reservoir for a great loop that takes 3 to 5 hours. Use extreme caution, especially near streams and along the shoreline.

Tours south of Route 2

On the following pages we present some of the well-known tours south of Route 2. Most of them use the **Catamount Trail**. We conclude the chapter with a few tours in the northern-most part of the state. Consult the *Catamount Trail Guidebook* (1995) for detailed trail descriptions.

Honey Hollow (Camel's Hump north side)

This north–facing basin is a favorite section of the Catamount Trail. As it is in somewhat remote terrain, and the initial part of the descent has steep, narrow sections, the tour is advanced. Usually accessed from Camel's Hump Nordic Ski Center in Huntington from the top of Logger's Loop ski run, the 5–mile trail descends 1,600' to the Winooski River in Jonesville. It is easier to ski up the trail and then back to your car. Park on River Rd., 2.5 miles east of the Jonesville bridge.

Huntington Gap

The full version of this long tour starts from Mad River Barn (Waitsfield), ascends Phenn Basin and crosses the main ridge of the Green Mountains, before dropping steeply out of Huntington Gap and commencing a long northerly traverse above Huntington Valley (at about 1,500'), reaching Camel's Hump Nordic Ski Center after 15 miles. A 6–mile version of the route is to bail out at the first opportunity on the Huntington side, in Hanksville. Huntington Gap can be done as an out-and-back trip by using the excellent snowmobile trail from the end of Trapp Road, above Huntington Center.

Catamount Ski Trail

The Catamount Trail is a Vermont end-to-end cross
country ski trail that roughly parallels the Long Trail.
Conceived in 1982, the Catamount Trail is still under
development, with the route not finalized in some areas.
By the winter of 1996, about 90% of the 280 miles were
available for use. The Catamount Trail is generally at
much lower elevations than the Long Trail. Thus, instead
of running along the high ridges of the Green Mountains,
it seeks out skiable backcountry routes, which link the
various ski centers together. For example, from below
Middlebury Gap, the route runs north on unplowed
roads over Lincoln Gap, then along the bases of the
Sugarbush downhill ski areas, before again crossing the
main ridge. It then continues north along the west flank
of Camel's Hump to Bolton Valley and on to Stowe.

Blueberry Hill (Goshen) to Breadloaf (Ripton)

A 9.5-mile ski over moderate, gently rolling terrain from the
cross county ski area at the Blueberry Hill Inn to the Rickert
Ski Center on Route 125, a short distance from Middlebury.
The trail is done in either direction or as a round trip, and it
is a very accessible and popular segment of the Catamount
Trail. This is an excellent trail for skiers wanting to try out the
backcountry. South of Blueberry Hill, the trail continues to
Goshen. A fine variation through Leicester Hollow takes you
directly to the Churchill House Inn on Route 73 in Goshen.

Somerset Reservoir

This relatively remote section of the Catamount Trail runs
along the east shore of Somerset Reservoir, deep in the

Skiers on the Catamount Trail

National Forest. From parking on Kelley Stand Road (south of Stratton Mountain), the trail heads south on the access road to Grout Pond, passing the pond to the west. Continuing south, it soon reaches Somerset Reservoir and runs along its east side, reaching the dam (and access road) at the south end, for a total distance of 7.5 miles. Grout Pond has a network of ski trails and a cabin available for winter use.

Hazen's Notch–Jay Pass area

Skiing through Hazen's Notch on the unplowed Bailey Hazen Military Road (Route 58) has long been a favorite ski tour in the north country. After the fine and fast 500'-descent from Hazen's Notch (1,800'), the trail leads to Hazen's Notch Nordic Center. Continuing north, there is excellent skiing up to Jay Pass where there are good views. From the pass a fine, rolling descent to Jay village awaits.

Backpacking along the Long Trail

The following pages offer some introductory backpacking hikes on the Long Trail. If you're interested in a description of the entire Long Trail, consult the Green Mountain Club's **Long Trail Guide**.

From Johnson north to Rte. 118; 20 miles, 3 days.

From Route 15, about 2 miles west of Johnson, the Long Trail north to Route 118 provides a remote hike in the peaceful north woods of Vermont. This is a great introductory backpack, popular with families. Three cabins provide shelter. From **Ithiel Falls Camp** (0.9 mile west on Hogback Rd.), follow the LT up and over **Prospect Rock** (good views of the Lamoille Valley). Continue across moderate terrain, soon reaching **Roundtop Shelter** (3-sided shelter, space for 8), at 2.5 miles, for a short first day. Onwards, after crossing the Johnson–Waterville Road, make a short climb before descending into Codding Hollow. Then head right on the road and climb to **Laraway Lookout** (2,620') with its view south to the Mt. Mansfield area. Continue over Laraway Mountain and on to **Corliss Camp**, 8 miles from Roundtop Shelter. Stop at Corliss Camp, with bunk space for 12. From Corliss, it is a little over a mile to the top of Butternut Mountain (partial view), and a total of 7.3 miles to **Ritterbush Camp**, room for 8, (overlooking a lovely stream), or 9.6 miles to Rt. 118. Just before Ritterbush Camp, you pass through rocky, secluded **Devil's Gulch**. In May, you'll see purple trillium. As an added bonus on your last day, park your packs, cross Rt. 118, and follow the LT up **Belvidere Mtn.** (3,360'). A 0.2–mile spur trail (right) leads to the top. The tower provides one of the most dramatic mountain views in this part of Vermont. Round trip is 5.6 miles; elevation gain is 2,140'.

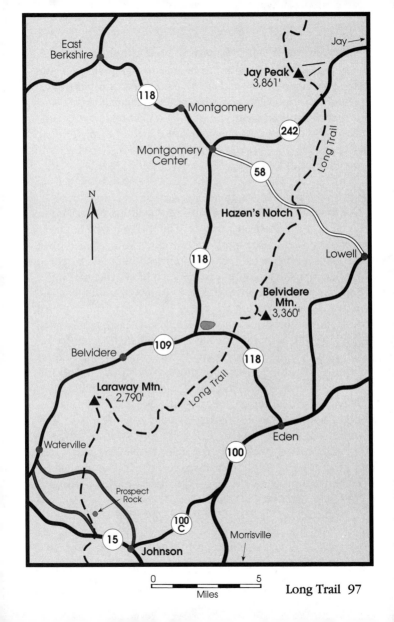

East
Berkshire

118

Montgomery

Montgomery
Center

Jay →

Jay Peak
3,861'

242

58

Hazen's Notch

Long Trail

N

Lowell

118

Belvidere
Mtn.
3,360'

109

Belvidere

118

Laraway Mtn.
2,790'

Long Trail

Waterville

Eden

100

Prospect
Rock

100
C

Morrisville
↓

15

Johnson

0   5
Miles

Long Trail 97

Traverse of Mount Mansfield, 1–3 days

For many, this 10-mile traverse of the long ridge of our highest mountain from Lake Mansfield north to Smugglers Notch is Vermont's most rugged and spectacular hike. Sweeping views, an exciting two miles of trail above treeline, and some difficult climbs make this a memorable outing. The trip is done in either direction and with variations. To reach the trailhead for **Taylor Lodge**, drive to the end of Nebraska Valley from Stowe. Hike in past the Lake Mansfield Trout Club (private), and walk along the lake before climbing steeply to the lodge (space for 20) and the Long Trail at 1.6 miles. After avoiding **Nebraska Notch** proper (a jumble of huge boulders), the LT traverses the west flank of Dewey Mtn., passing **Twin Brooks** tenting area 2 miles from Taylor Lodge and reaching the short trail left to **Butler Lodge** 1.3 miles farther on. Butler (space for 14) is nicely perched high on the mountain. The next day return to the Long Trail and ascend the exposed slabs of the **Forehead** (use protected Forehead Bypass in bad weather). From the top of the Forehead, it is 2 miles to the **Chin** (main summit), most of which is along the open summit ridge. On the way, an ascent of the **Nose** is recommended. The Triangle Trail ascends the steep rocks to the top, 0.2 mile. Now walk the long, gentle summit ridge to the mountain's highest point. After enjoying the views, descend to Taft either via the somewhat exposed LT (0.4 mile), or if the weather is bad, backtrack (0.2 mile) to the **Profanity Trail**, which drops (left) directly down to Taft. Taft Lodge will be rebuilt in the summer of 1996. From the lodge down to Route 108, it is a pleasant 1.7 miles.

Distance: 10.7 miles, climbing: 4,000' (includes Nose)

Maps: Hiker's Guide to Mt. Mansfield; Trail Map of Mt. Mansfield; USGS Mt. Mansfield, 1:24 000 and 1:100 000.

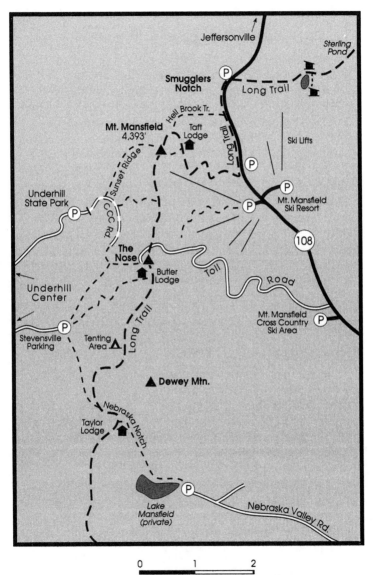

Jeffersonville

Sterling Pond

Smugglers Notch

Long Trail

Hell Brook Tr.

Mt. Mansfield 4,393'

Taft Lodge

Long Trail

Ski Lifts

Sunset Ridge

Underhill State Park

CCC Rd.

Mt. Mansfield Ski Resort

108

The Nose

Butler Lodge

Underhill Center

Toll Road

Long Trail

Stevensville Parking

Tenting Area

Mt. Mansfield Cross Country Ski Area

▲ Dewey Mtn.

Taylor Lodge

Nebraska Notch

Lake Mansfield (private)

Nebraska Valley Rd.

0   1   2
Miles

Long Trail 99

Griffith Lake Loop, 2 days

This loop trip past peaceful Griffith Lake uses the Long Trail as one side of the loop. From F.S. Rd. #10, the AT/LT (south) does a pleasant descending traverse to **Big Branch Shelter** (1.4 miles), crosses a suspension bridge, and reaches the **Old Job Trail** at 1.5 miles. Head left on Old Job, passing **Old Job Shelter** after a mile, and crossing F.S. Rd. #30 after another mile. From here it is 3.3 miles on to Griffith Lake and the Long Trail. At the lake head *south* (left) 0.7 mile on the LT to **Peru Peak Shelter** (space for 10). Day 1 is 7.5 miles. On day 2, follow the LT north back past Griffith Lake and make the climb up and over **Baker Peak** (at 2.5 miles) with its fine views of the "Valley of Vermont". Continuing north over moderate terrain, the LT reaches **Lost Pond Shelter** (space for 8), at 4.5 miles. Then it's another 2.8 miles back past Big Branch Shelter to F.S. Rd. #10 and your starting point. Day 2 is 7.3 miles.

Total distance: 14.8 miles, total climbing: 1,900'

Approach: From Danby (Rt. 7), drive 3.5 miles up F.S. Rd. #10, where the AT/LT heads south (right), and park.

Little Rock Pond

An easy 2-mile hike north on the LT (and AT) from Mt. Tabor Road brings you to beautiful and very popular Little Rock Pond. **Lula Tye Shelter** is just before the pond and **Little Rock Shelter** just north of it—both have space for about eight. At the northern end of the pond, 0.4 mile farther on, the blue-blazed **Green Mountain Trail** (branches left) leads up to a great viewpoint over the pond, about a half mile away. Return by the same route or by the using the side trail that completes the loop around the west side of the pond.

Total distance: 6 miles, total climb: 1,000'

Approach: Trailhead parking is 3.4 miles up Mt. Tabor Road.

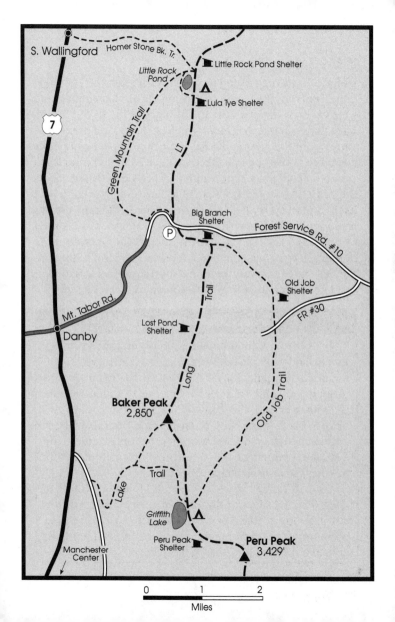

S. Wallingford

Homer Stone Bk. Tr.

Little Rock Pond Shelter

Little Rock Pond

Lula Tye Shelter

7

Green Mountain Trail

LT

Big Branch Shelter

P

Forest Service Rd. #10

Trail

Old Job Shelter

FR #30

Mt. Tabor Rd.

Danby

Lost Pond Shelter

Long

Old Job Trail

Baker Peak
2,850'

Trail

Lake

Griffith Lake

Peru Peak Shelter

Peru Peak
3,429'

Manchester Center

0   1   2
Miles

The Long Trail

Unique for its rugged and unspoiled character, the 265-mile Long Trail runs the length of Vermont, from Massachusetts to Canada. As it traverses the main ridges of the Green Mountains, it passes over Vermont's highest peaks, and the terrain varies from rocky summits above treeline to peaceful ponds and lakes. Along the trail there are over 70 shelters and small cabins (called "lodges" or "camps"). The side trails that access the Long Trail are marked with blue blazes, and the Long Trail itself is marked with white blazes. The 2,100-mile **Appalachian Trail**, which runs from Georgia to Maine, was inspired by the Long Trail. For 100 miles north from the Massachusetts border, the two trails coincide. A few miles north of Killington, the "AT" turns eastward, entering New Hampshire at Hanover, and after traversing the White Mountains, enters Maine.

Green Mountain Club

The Green Mountain Club is Vermont's primary hiking and backpacking organization with over 6,500 members. The mission of the GMC is to "maintain and protect the Long Trail", including the 175 miles of side trails that access the Long Trail. These side trails are heavily used, since they often provide the most direct approach to the summits. As a non-profit organization, the GMC is dependent on the volunteer efforts of its members to keep the trails in shape.

In recent years, the Green Mountain Club has been working successfully to permanently protect northern sections of the Long Trail, which face increasing pressure from development; thus the club is helping to preserve the trail for future generations.

United States Forest Service

In Vermont, the U.S. Forest Service administers the **Green Mountain National Forest (GMNF)**, an area of about 340,000 acres. It is made up of three districts, Middlebury, Rochester, and Manchester. The Supervisor' s Office is in Rutland. All four locations have visitor centers with a variety of maps and informative pamphlets, most of which are free of charge.

Recreation and timber/wildlife management make up the program of work for the Forest Service. An extensive system of numbered Forest Roads provides good access to the mountains and trails. There are hundreds of miles of maintained hiking trails in the Green Mountain National Forest, and the trail and road signs are generally excellent.

Approximately one-sixth of the GMNF acreage is designated as wilderness, with the Lye Brook Wilderness near Manchester and Stratton the largest wilderness area. These areas offer excellent opportunities for exploratory hiking, camping, bird watching, and wildlife enjoyment.

Dept. of Forests, Parks and Recreation

The Vermont Department of Forests, Parks and Recreation manages our state park system. The parks are ideal starting points for many of the hikes in this guide. There are good camping facilities near Mount Mansfield, Mount Hunger, Mount Ascutney, Lake Dunmore and Middlebury, Manchester and Stratton, the Mount Snow area, Groton State Forest, and the Northeast Kingdom. Telephone and address information appears later in this section.

USGS Topographic Map Sources

The area code for Vermont is 802.

Capitol Stationers, Main Street, Montpelier	223-2393
Climb High, Shelburne Road, Shelburne	985-5055
Eastern Mountain Sports, South Burlington	864-0473
Mink Brook Outfitters, West Lebanon, NH	603-298-7840
Mountain Goat, Route 7A, Manchester Center	362-5159
The National Survey, Chester	875-2121
Northern Cartographic, South Burlington	860-2886
Tempest Book Shop, Waitsfield	496-2022
Vermont Book Shop, Main Street, Middlebury	388-6991

Other Maps

Trail map of Mount Mansfield, 1995, $3.95, Topographic map of Mount Mansfield showing approach roads. All hiking trails are given a difficulty rating. Published by the Green Mountain Club.

Hiker's Guide to Mount Mansfield, 1996, $4.95. Bird's-eye view drawing of Mount Mansfield, in color. Descriptions of the main hiking routes and other useful information about the mountain. Published by Huntington Graphics.

Green Mountain National Forest Map, 1984, $3.00 each Color maps of the National Forest: A northern and a southern section are provided. Shows towns, roads, elevations, and trails. Available at F.S. district offices.

Vermont Road Atlas and Guide, 1995, $15.95. Detailed road coverage, with topography shown in color. Helpful in locating the trailheads; hiking trails are shown. Published by Northern Cartographic.

Guide books

Long Trail Guide, 238 pages, 1996. GMC Covers the 265-mile Long Trail and the 175 miles of trails that access it. Includes a topographic map of Mount Mansfield and Camel's Hump. $14.95

Fifty Hikes in Vermont, 192 pages, 1991. GMC Walks and hikes discussed at some length. Historical and anecdotal information. Excellent for beginners. $12.00

Best Hikes with Children in Vermont, New Hampshire & Maine, 258 pages, 1991. Cynthia Lewis. Published by the Mountaineers, Seattle. Thorough descriptions of hikes suitable for children. $12.95

Guide to Adirondack Trails: High Peaks Region, 324 pages, 1992. The Adirondack Mountain Club, Glens Falls, NY, publishes comprehensive hiking guides for the seven different regions of the Adirondacks in New York. $16.95

AMC White Mountain Guide, 638 pages, 1992. Appalachian Mountain Club, Boston, MA. Complete hikers guide to the White Mountains of New Hampshire. $16.95

Catamount Trail Guidebook, 104 pages, 1995. Published by the Catamount Trail Association, Burlington, VT. Comprehensive guide, with topo maps, to Vermont's 280-mile end-to-end backcountry ski trail.

Classic Backcountry Skiing: *A Guide to the Best Ski Tours in New England*, 298 pages, 1989. David Goodman. Published by the AMC, Boston. $11.95

Hiking and Trail Organizations

Green Mountain Club
RR1 Box 650, Waterbury Center, VT 05677   244-7037
The club office and Gameroff Hiker Center are located on
Route 100, about 4 miles north of Interstate 89.

Vermont Dept. of Forests, Parks and Recreation,
103 South Main St., Waterbury, VT 05676   244-8711
Maintains trails, campgrounds, and picnic areas in state
forests and parks. Various free local trail maps.

Green Mountain National Forest, Supervisor's Office
The Visitor Center is on Route 7 in Rutland.   747-6700
District offices in Middlebury, Manchester, and Rochester.
Maintains trails and recreation facilities in the national
forest. Free area brochures and maps are available.

Catamount Trail Association
P.O Box 1235, Burlington, VT 05402   864-5794
Membership organization formed to develop and maintain
Vermont's 280-mile end-to-end cross country ski trail.

Youth Corps (Vermont Youth Conservation Corps)
P.O Box 482, Waterbury, VT 05676   241-3906
Youth service organization that carries out trail building
and maintenance and various other conservation projects.

Ascutney Trails Association
P.O. Box 147, Windsor, VT 05089
The ATA publishes the Mount Ascutney Guide.

Westmore Association Trail Committee, Westmore, VT
Maintains hiking trails in the Lake Willoughby area.

Index

Mount Abraham 38-40
Alpine Trail (Camel's Hump) 33,34
Appalachian Gap 40
Appalachian Trail 50,100,102
Mount Ascutney 55-58

Baker Peak 64,100
Balanced Rock 31
Bald Mountain (Bennington) 67
Bald Mountain (Townshend) 72
Bald Mountain (Westmore) 84
Bamforth Ridge Trail (Camel's Hump) 34
Bascom Lodge (Mt. Greylock) 68
Battell Mountain 47
Battell Shelter and Trail (Mt. Abraham) ... 38,39
Beaver Meadow Lodge 22
Belvidere Mountain 79,96
Big Deer Mountain 75
Black Swamp Trail (Shrewsbury Peak) 52
Blue Ridge Mountain 54
Bolton To Trapps Ski Trail 88
Bolton Mountain 23,90
Bolton Valley Ski Area 88
Branbury State Park 48
Brandon Gap 49
Breadloaf Mountain 45,47
Bromley Mountain 64
Brownsville Trail (Mt. Ascutney) 55
Bruce Ski Trail 92
Bryant Lodge 88
Buchanan Mountain 80
Bucklin Trail (Killington Peak) 50
Burke Mountain 87

Burnt Mountain 80
Burrows Trail (Camel's Hump) 32
Burt Ski Trail 90
Butler Lodge 20,98

CCC Road (Mt. Mansfield) 18,19,91
Camel's Hump 32-37
Cantilever Rock 18
Canty Trail (Blue Ridge Mtn.) 54
Cape Lookout Mountain 49
Mount Cardigan (NH) 58
Catamount Ski Trail 37,48,93,94
Catamount Trail Association 95
Chin (Mt. Mansfield) 12-20,98
Cooley Glen Shelter 45
Cooper Lodge 50,51
Corliss Camp 96
Cottonbrook Basin 90

Dean Trail (Camel's Hump) 33,34
Deer Leap Rock 52
Devil's Gulch 96
Dewey Mountain 22
Dewey Saddle 90
The Dome 68
Dorset Peak 65
Lake Dunmore 48

Elephant's Head 21
Mount Ellen 40
Mount Elmore 31
Emily Proctor Shelter 45
Mount Equinox 60

Falls of Lana 48
Forehead (Mt. Mansfield) 20,98
Forest City Trail (Camel's Hump) 32
Forestry Trail (Camel's Hump) 33,34
Frost Trail (Mt. Mansfield) 20
Futures Trail (Mt. Ascutney) 57

General Stark Mountain 42
Glastenbury Mountain 67
Glen Ellen Lodge 40
Goddard Shelter 67
Gorham Lodge 34,36
Mount Grant 45
Green Mountain Club 30,78,102
Green Mountain Trail 100
Mount Greylock (Mass.) 68
Griffith Lake 64,100
Groton State Forest 75-77
Grout Pond 63,95

Halfway House Trail (Mt. Mansfield) 18
Harmon Hill 66
Haselton Trail 99
Harrington's View 23
Haystack Mountain (Westmore) 84
Haystack Mountain (Wilmington) 71
Haystack Pond 71
Hazen's Notch 95,97
Healdville Trail (Mt. Okemo) 58
Hell Brook Trail (Mt. Mansfield) 13
Honey Hollow Ski Trail 37,93
Hopper Trail (Mt. Greylock) 68
Mount Hor 83

Mount Horrid Overlook 49
Mount Hunger 26-28

Jay Peak 81
Jerusalem Trail (Mt. Ellen) 40

Kettle Pond Trail 77
Killington Peak 50,51

Laraway Mountain 78,96
Laura Cowles Trail (Mt. Mansfield) 19
Lincoln Gap 38,40
Little River State Park 92
Little Rock Pond 100
Long Trail 7,12,21,45,81,96-102
Lookout Rock 60
Lye Brook Falls 61

Maps 11,104
Mad River Glen Ski Area 42
Mad River Valley 38-43
Madonna Mountain 22
Maple Ridge and Trail (Mt. Mansfield) 20
Middlesex Trail (Mt. Hunger) 26,28
Mount Monadnock (Vermont) 86
Mount Monadnock (New Hampshire) 74
Montclair Glen Lodge 32
Morse Mountain 22
Lake Mansfield 98
Mount Mansfield 12-20,98
Mount Mansfield Cross Country Ski Area 88
Mount Moosalamoo 48

Nebraska Notch 22,92,98

Nebraska Valley 90
Needle's Eye 98
Nose (Mt. Mansfield) 14,15,20,98

Old Job Trail 100
Mount Okemo 58
Mount Olga 72
Owl's Head 75

Pico Peak 51
Mount Pisgah 82
Profanity Trail (Mt. Mansfield) 12
Prospect Rock (Johnson) 78,96
Prospect Rock (Manchester) 61
Pulpit Rock 82

Ranch Valley 90
Rattlesnake Point 48
Ricker Mountain 23
Ritterbush Camp 96
Robert Frost Lookout 47
Roundtop Shelter 96

Sherburne Pass 51,52
Shrewsbury Peak 52
Skiing 37,48,70,77,88-95
Skylight Pond and Trail 47
Skyline Lodge 47
Skyline Ridge Trail (Mt. Hunger) 27,28
Skytop Ski Trail 90
Smugglers Notch 21,88
Snake Mountain 44
Mount Snow 70
Somerset Reservoir 94
Spruce Mountain (Groton S. F.) 77

Spruce Peak (Manchester) 62
Stark's Nest 40,42
Sterling Pond 21
Stowe Pinnacle 27,28
Stratton Mountain 62
Stratton Pond 62
Sugarbush Ski Area 40
Sunset Ledge 38
Sunset Ridge (Mt. Mansfield) 18

Taconic Range 60
Taft Lodge 12,13,98
Taylor Lodge 22,98
Teardrop Ski Trail 92
Toll Road (Mt. Mansfield) 14
Mount Tom 59
Trapp Cabin 90
Trapp Family Lodge 88

Underhill State Park 18,19,91
Underhill Ski Trail 90

Mount Wantastiquet (NH) 72
Waterbury Reservoir 92
W.B. Ski Trail 91
Weathersfield Trail (Mt. Ascutney) 56
Wheeler Mountain 84
White Rock Mountain 26
White Rock Trail (Mt. Hunger) 26,28
Whiteface Mountain 22
Lake Willoughby 82
Wind Gap 32,34,37
Windsor Trail (Mt. Ascutney) 55,58
Mount Worcester 30
Worcester Range 26-31
Worth Mountain 47